Say What Loneliness?

Say What Loneliness?

Chaunda Gaines

Copyright © Chaunda Gaines.

All rights reserved. No part of this book may be reproduced in any form or by any electronic or mechanical means, including information storage and retrieval systems, without permission in writing from the publisher, except by reviewers, who may quote brief passages in a review.

ISBN: 978-1-64826-529-7 (Paperback Edition)
ISBN: 978-1-64826-530-3 (Hardcover Edition)
ISBN: 978-1-64826-528-0 (E-book Edition)

Some characters and events in this book are fictitious. Any similarity to real persons, living or dead, is coincidental and not intended by the author.

Book Ordering Information

Phone Number: 347-901-4929 or 347-901-4920
Email: info@globalsummithouse.com
Global Summit House
www.globalsummithouse.com

Printed in the United States of America

CONTENTS

Introduction vii

Breakup 1
Adult/Teen Suicide 4
Drifters 8
Actor 11
Foster/Adoptive Parent 14
Elderly (An Alzheimer's Person) 17
Married Person 20
Sex 24
Isolation 26
Incarceration 28
Workaholic 32
Drug Addiction/Alcoholic 35
Dating Game 39
Deceased Loved One 43
Separation 47
Triumph of War 50
Rape 53
Holiday Season 56
Financial Difficulty 60
Aging 63

Conclusion 67
Poem For Your Thoughts 70

INTRODUCTION

My name is Chaunda Gaines. I'm a self help author who keeps it real, simple and plain. That's my mo "rsp" that's me. I write about real life issues and problems that we face in our everyday life. I was born and raised in Third Ward, Texas with one brother and one sister. I went to a private school. I'm single, raised two wonderful behaving daughters in which I was always there for them as they were growing up. I gave good advice as a mother in order for them not to make the same mistakes I made. I'm a person of color who realized you have to be unique or gifted at something to stand out from the rest to succeed in life. I'm the middle child in my family; often treated like the black sheep of the family, that I am nothing nor will I ever amount to anything. This enabled me to have drive and determination to fulfill my dream and vision of becoming a writer. I had nobody there for me in my life but the good lord above who watched over me as I was growing up. I went through plenty of storms, failed relationships and marriages. I was sheltered as a young girl so I grew up finding out about life the hard way. If I had someone to tell me about life, I wouldn't have made so many mistakes in my life to begin with. So I began to write to help others find solutions to the many questions that pop up in their minds that they may not want to share with someone and how to deal with the life they have now in which they have made good or bad choices in which they're living with. I keep my writings real and don't sugarcoat my words. I'm not cutting any corners in the way I write. I will bring it to you like it should be. A lot of times we don't have solutions and answers to a lot of problems and issues we go through. I try to bring out your innermost feelings and thoughts in so many different ways and angles on how we maybe feeling about situations in our life where we are misunderstood by others. Sometimes that's not what we are trying to say when we are talking about what's going on with our lives. As I was growing up, loneliness always surrounded me in some shape, form or fashion. I could not put it together until I became older. I'm sure you're probably thinking, "She's writing about loneliness. Oh how sad?" or "What does she know about that topic?" Let me inform you. I feel some higher being or spirit has led me to write this book on this particular topic to help someone out there who just doesn't know why they do some things that end up hurting themselves or someone else. Loneliness can be derived from so many areas in our life that we, as individuals, may not even be aware of. As you continue to read this book, I hope you can find out where loneliness fits into your life. Do you have a solution? Do you know of someone who self-consciously may have a problem of loneliness? Does your behavior play a part in your loneliness? After reading this book, if you know of someone, buy this book for them or for yourself. See if you can make your life better than what it is. See if it can bring you back your self-confidence and assurance in your life that you could have lost down the road and don't know why. Now let's go over some things loneliness deals with. What the definitions could be that you may never have even thought about. Loneliness can also be a deep, dark, empty feeling inside your soul, never letting go of your emotions that's trapped inside of you or loneliness can mean that you can be trapped into a world of the unknown depending upon your state of mind. Being trapped could mean being in your own zone or seclusion where it's just you and nobody else to bother you. You could be in a room, just you and complete darkness staring in space or you could be sitting at the table with earplugs in your ear listening to music in your own zone tuning everybody out or in the computer surfing the website or in a chat room in your own zone or world. All of this can also be associated with loneliness; singling oneself from others than being in the company of people or maybe you can be in deep thought or concentration of trying to put your life into prospective. You can be lonely just in your house doing nothing or maybe sitting in a corner with your knees bent Indian style with your head between your legs, maybe wishing for someone to stop by or knock at your door or call you on the phone. You can be on the freeway. You see a car next to you and wave at that person or maybe you try to get that person to pull over so you can get his/her number or introduce yourself. What possesses a person to flag a car down? Get that person's number: loneliness! Because no one may be in your life. Had you thought of decision making? Making decisions hastily, everyone has done this sometime or another in their life. Decision making can resolve problems/situations that come up in your daily life. When making decisions, you seriously analyze that issue step by step, weigh all the different angles carefully and scrutinize that problem like the man in the mirror. Decisions that individuals make can really affect the outcome of their life in particular being wrong or right. If you make a wrong decision it can cause you to crawl up in a nut shell excluding yourself from everyone because of that decision you made. What outcome that can come from this? Loneliness hopes that no erratic behavior comes from it such as: committing suicide, drug addiction, killing someone, going clubbing by oneself, going on blind dates, physical & sexual abusers, rapists, traveling & vacationing by oneself, adoption, hypochondria, alcoholic, trusting someone that you know and feel may not have your best interest at heart. All the things above are associated with loneliness in some shape, form or fashion. If you dig deep inside and think about it, there could be more things that I haven't touched on that you individually may know of with oneself that loneliness plays a part of where you are concerned. Thought process hun. Many times in our lives we've done things that just didn't make sense or add up. Then we ask ourselves why did I do this? or what lead me to do this? As you continue to read this book, I hope it can help you to see where change may be needed in your life. Rethink how you live your life and see how you can reorganize it for the better if loneliness exists there. Making adjustments in your life is always good because there's always room for improvement in our daily life. Remember if you have a problem in life it can always be fixed and worked out with a solution. Believe that! These are short topics that are precise examples or real life issues that we are faced with in our everyday life to help you think about how you're living if loneliness is present. Who knows you could change for the better or you could feel fine just the way you are.

BREAKUP

My main squeeze broke up with me today. All of a sudden I became lonely inside of my heart. It was just like someone took a knife and stabbed me over & over again until I became numb and couldn't feel anymore. When someone says love hurts, it does, make no mistake about it. I just cried, crocodile tears rolling down my face. Make no mistake about it. It's just out of control; leaving you empty and destroying whatever love that was inside you to give to someone else. You know what else, it leaves you soooo lonely: no one to visit you, to love you, to hug you, to argue with, fight with, to talk to like you would with your man or woman. Now you have to cope all over again, to learn to date once again. If you're a person that's in only one relationship at a time, you got to start all over again like a baby taking their first step. It's hard to move on without the person you are in love with because you heard from your grandparents that love only comes once in a lifetime. If you get that kind of love, you better hold onto it and do whatever you have to do to keep it. Now loneliness steps in. Guess what a lonely person can do that's foolish and stupid? Go to a friend house and knock on that person's door just to see if they could enjoy each other's company. See where it could lead: you know a friend to talk too, listen to music with, watch some television with, cry with, tell your problems too, lay your head on his/her shoulders. You know, kick it with but no sex involved. You may have thought he/she may have wanted to get to know you better but may not. What if you had that person number stored in your call list from your cell phone or your caller ID from your telephone? Because he/she rejected you like your main squeeze did, you always may think about in your mind that you're not going to have anything to do with that person because of fear he/she doesn't want to go through that pain again. So you delete that person's number from your cell phone or telephone like it's nothing. This action shows how really hurt you are. This is what loneliness can cause you to do. But you know what, just laugh at the way you handled that incident. If you laugh you can get a beautiful smile out of it. But know loneliness will still be there. There will still be emptiness in your heart that will continue to hurt because you're not with the one you love. When you go through something like this, you still miss that one true man/woman you always dreamed of having the most in your life. But you still have to keep it real with yourself. Tell yourself that he/she didn't want you. You could be the perfect man/woman that never argued with your loved one, had dinner ready and prepared for them, the house cleaned spotless, made passionate love to him/her however that person wanted it whether it was from the front or the back door, jumped up like a robot when he called your name. What more could a person want from a loved one? By doing all the things mention above, you know you did all you can do to keep that relationship together. This right here can bring about loneliness creeping up on you like Freddy Krueger, ripping out your heart with his/her long iron nails. If you don't know how to cope, you could very well commit suicide or kill that person for causing you sooo much pain, grief and sorrow inside or just be plain miserable for the rest of your life; never getting over the breakup of that loved person or you can just pray about it to the good lord, go to church on a regular basis developing a relationship with God instead of being just an acquaintance or a seat warmer which includes getting involved in church activities which will keep you busy and your mind free from wander. You know that person is not worthy of the type of love you have given him/her. If you think about it, the person you loved is not losing one ounce of sleep over you and crying crocodile tears over you but has moved on with their life with somebody else. But they will lead you to believe that they are not with anyone if that relationship doesn't work out with the person that they are dating. So you can have a little hope or faith that they just might come back to you. Don't believe the game. Keep your head and chin up. Believe in yourself! Believe that you can make it through this tough storm or the rain even though it's tough. There's an old saying, when the going gets tough, the tough gets going. The tough smoothes out and it's no more tough. Believe that whatever you go through, know and have faith that God will see you through this victoriously. Just know that God has something better in store for you. It could be right around the corner. Realize that man just didn't want you. He/she broke up with you for all the wrong reasons making it seem like everything was your fault but it's not. The only thing he/she wanted to do was his/her own thing. You know what? That man/woman probably wasn't for you anyway. You didn't want to come to terms with that. Just wait and be patient. The right person will come into your life and treat you right. You don't have to go looking for him/her. Believe that! The right person will find you.

ADULT/TEEN SUICIDE

What can cause a grown person to take their life? You think that loneliness could have played a part or could it be that there was just no way out. I always believe that loneliness plays a big part whether we believe it or not. We sometimes know it but don't want to accept it. I know a person wanted to kill herself because she likes women. That person was living her life in the closet, not wanting anybody to know about it, keeping their life on the down low. Their daughter didn't even tell her own parents, brothers, sisters, cousins or aunties, but one day her mother started snooping around in her room going through her dresser drawers, clothes in the closet, boxes and shoes, bags of miscellaneous stuff in her room and came upon a letter. This letter contained information about her relationship with a woman. The mother started reading it and stumbled on the fact that her daughter was in a relationship with a woman; that's why she went to her prom with a girl, that's why no boy came to the house, that's why all her friends was girls. Everything added up and started making sense. The mother became upset as she kept dwelling on it and ran and showed her husband the letter. He became furious to know that his only daughter likes a woman instead of a man. Everyday for weeks and months, mom and dad were always fussing at her and cursing her out every time they thought about it or even when it just popped up in their minds. They started threatening to beat the hell out of her if she didn't end her relationship with that woman and change her lifestyle. Now the daughter that liked her female companionship felt like she didn't have anybody there for her in her corner. She felt alone because her life was out in the open. She wasn't ready to tell anyone yet especially her parents. You know sometimes parents can evade your privacy. They get too anxious;

they start to sense something is not right but they just don't know what. That's when they will go in that child's room and start snooping because they pay the bills. Now wait after they do this, then they go to that telephone. That's it! They're calling everybody they can tell. Now everybody knows her business. How can she face this now that everyone knows? Now, out of the blue, loneliness creeps in and she starts crawling up in her own shell blocking everybody out because of the constant battle with her parents—rating her low and humiliating her. She felt alone again like she didn't have a friend in the world that could understand her situation. She wanted her parents to accept her lifestyle but they wouldn't. So they told her if she was to continue to stay at home, she could not bring her lover to their house. Her lover also could not come over for the holidays and they did not want to meet her. They wanted to see their only daughter with a man and to give them grandchildren. Now this could never happen because she's gay. Because of the constant bickering with her parents, she felt alone and with no one to understand or accept her situation. She contemplated taking her life many times; not knowing how to deal with this type of situation. When your parents don't accept your way of life it hurts deep inside cause they can't share in your happiness. You know when a child becomes grown, we have to let our child go into the world. Let them experience life. This is hard to do because we want them to stay a child forever. You want your parent as your best friend. It's sad when your child wants to take their life because of the key word acceptance. That's real loneliness. No one to listens to them or hears their cry. But you parents out there, needs to accept your child's lifestyle whether male or female. I know it's hard and the Bible teaches against it, if you're religious. But what if your child married a man or had a male boyfriend that person gave her AIDS or hepatitis C that caused her death. Then she died unhappy, unhappy of not being with that person she truly loved. Be open-minded because you can save that child's life by letting them be happy with their choices of love because you, the parents, have lived your life how you wanted to. I know the Bible condemns this kind of relationship. You know God wants us to be happy and to be loved. God forgives everyone for their sins because Christ died for us. Here's another situation of adult suicide that resulted from being lonely. A person loses their job, then their house, their car and then the man/woman left them because everything was gone. No more material things or possessions to keep them there. That person didn't have anybody to turn to. Even his/her dad or mom, sister and brother turned their backs and told the man/woman they couldn't come to their house to live. The children wouldn't let their mom/dad come to stay with them and they had apartments. So what happened was, he/she started living on the streets. He/she lost everything; his/her whole life, self esteem and his/her dignity. He/she used to be a strong woman/man; succeeded in everything he/she set his/her mind too. He/she was raped, beaten, cut up, lived on the streets, slept in abandoned houses, apartments, junkyards, under the freeway and even made a box and had a mattress that he/she slept on, where you would always hear sounds of cars driving by—he/she really had it hard. You know that that person was really alone. All of his/her friends and family turned their backs on him/her. He/she always was a loving, kind person that always helped everyone that he/she could; financially and emotionally. Now, believe it or not, this person was completely by himself/herself. Loneliness hun! Nobody's there for him/her! How sad! There's a lesson to be learned here. God blesses those that help other people. That's where your blessing comes from. If someone falls, pick them up if they're a friend or family member because one day you could end up in that person's shoes. If you are a professed Christian, do the right thing and open up your house for that person. Don't think that your house is too much for someone to stay in, that they may steal your jewelry or your finest possessions because your house could burn down or flood could happen. Never worship material things; they could be taken away from you like a thief in the night. By all means don't let someone close to you stand alone and end up on the streets. Have love and compassion for someone in need. Don't let them fall! Just one more thing, loneliness can make a person kill themselves. Because no one is there to pick them up when they fall. If you know of someone or are aware of someone in this situation, God does expect you to be there for that person because it could come back to haunt you in some form shape, or fashion in your life. Things could start going bad for you because you didn't do the right thing to help. There's also another form of suicide, and that's teen suicide, that's so popular today. A form of suicide that is not being accepted by your peers or the hood you grew up in. Some kids commit suicide in packs or groups—not giving life a chance. Some of you get unnoticed because your parents work two and three jobs to make ends meet. You're starving for some attention from your parents but nobody's there for you. Who can teens turn to? Where can they go? Who can question what they do? To help a suicide person we need to recognize that person's state of mind and condition that he/she is in. We just need to take a little time from our busy schedule and just notice our children for a quick minute or two. That just may make all the difference in the world. We parents should pay attention to our children and help them to fit into their society so they won't take their lives. We parents should go where our kids want us to go sometimes; not all the time. Let them know some places are restricted for children or teens. Let your child know what some kids do may not be good for them. Visit their world for just a little bit. Point out things in their world that could hinder them. This will make all the difference in the world. Just remember a suicide person withdraw themselves from everyone that may be close to them. We, as parents, need to recognize this in order to save them from hurting themselves. We, as parents, need to try to feel what they are feeling these days. Preteens and children today like to grow up too fast in that in crowd. We parents need to block out what mistakes we made in our life; stop blaming our kids for everything we didn't do with our lives. Whether it was not going to college or we may have gotten pregnant or had to dropped out of school, didn't go to the pro's, did drugs, and didn't know how to read, talk or write. We don't need to think our children will make the same mistake as we did. But trust them completely because you just might save their lives.

DRIFTERS

A drifter is a person that can't stay in one place at one time. A drifter may feel abandoned or deserted in his/her life. What if a drifter was in your neighborhood just driving through; notice a house with kids playing in the backyard during the daytime, scoping out your house thoroughly seeing every room in the house because there's no curtains on the windows, knowing where everybody's at because the lights are on. By all means make sure when night falls have a few lights on with your blinds closed. Usually drifters have driven from state to state and town to town. A drifter wanting company to fill his/her need. When everyone has gone to bed, the drifter snatches one of the kids or persons out of bed. It's all because they became lonely for someone—to be in their company. Loneliness can make you do a bad thing sometimes. Just maybe, this drifter needed a job to make a little money to pay for gas and food. The drifter may work probably one or two weeks even maybe a month. But he/she is scoping the neighborhood to take someone with him/her on his/her journey. Most kids that are taken by drifters end up being molested, raped and sometimes killed. They may not know how to handle this type of situation that they are in; when they're taken advantage of by a drifter or drifters. Sometimes you have to block everything out of your mind. So you won't have to feel the pain if the drifter takes advantage of you physically/sexually like Buddhism; sitting down Indian style, meditating your mind and body to be somewhere else, then you won't be able to feel the pain that the drifter is doing to you. When someone does you harm, it leaves your body very helpless and emotionally unbalanced because of being scared of what's going to happen to you next; you're not home where you feel safe. You don't have your parents to rescue or save you from that horrible person. You have to do whatever these drifters tell you to do from one day to the next; not knowing what will happen to you such as telling a lie, believing in it and living it because you're with someone else other than your parents who have always protected you from harm's way. You may even have to dye your hair, go by another name than your real name and make up another birthday and where you were born. They have to do this cause that drifter could kill them if the person/child doesn't do what they tell them. Sometimes a drifter's life, in their own minds, become complete because of taking someone that doesn't belong them because this could be a normal way of life for them. If the person runs away, they just go and get another child/person. Start the game all over again. It's sort of a sickness with the drifter or drifters. It's something they keep on doing until they get caught then they stop—maybe. They want to ask forgiveness for their sins but when you think about it's just an act of loneliness within. Maybe they wanted a family or they could be the only child. They could have been abused by their parents or could have been a nerd in school. Just doing something caused them to feel incomplete with themselves. This drifter needs professional help to talk maybe about problems that affect him in his/her childhood. The drifter may not know how to cope with what has happened to him/her in their earlier days. Sometimes, talking about something is good for the soul especially if your counselor/psychiatrist can help you on an individual basis. The counselor/psychiatrist can bring somethings out about you that you have not come to grips with. Things like this help you to recognize your own problems or issues in life. Say to oneself I really need help to overcome my bad problem. Sometimes loneliness can put a damper in your life; doing something you never thought you would do. You, as a drifter, need scrutinize yourself like the man in the mirror having the fear of the lord because murderers and evildoers will not inherit God's kingdom. Don't let that evil mind run away from you. If you don't believe in God, just remember how you grew up and you wouldn't want that for the person/child you took. By all means remember your mother or father did not actually raise you take something that doesn't belong to you. It's just like taking a cookie out of the cookie jar without permission. There's a parent out there that's panicking and freaking out about where's their child. Just maybe you don't have a heart or the fear of God within you or no conscious. Can you sympathize with the next person or with what the parent could be going through? Is there a way that you could feel their loss of a loved child? Could you even imagine what that parent could be going through? Remember, in the end a drifter usually gets caught eventually. Sometimes it's understandable that a drifter can't stay in one place too long to settle down and have a family; living in one place just all the time. If you lived where you went from place to place, that's how your life will end up following—on the go or on the run. If you want to change yourself from being a drifter, only you can do it. Stop the vicious cycle. Take a chance with life. You might be scared to do it but you never know until you take the first step. Having a family is beautiful; with the many trials, tribulation, storms and problems that comes with it. Taking something that belongs to someone else is horrible. It's like you're ripping that person's heart out. This parent is soo hurt with worry on where the child that they gave birth too or adopted can be.

ACTOR

When you think about an actor, lights, cameras and action comes to mind. This is the life of an entertainer; traveling all over the world doing a part in a script; all about getting that paper. But at what cost in their life. Acting is a very long exhausting, demanding job. You are away from your husband, children, friends and other relatives. Ask yourself, could this become associated with loneliness? Let's talk about acting. You're pretending to be another person in a script. You have to remember your lines. In doing this, it's hard to distinguish what's real or not when playing different roles or characters. Then you have to travel to a city where you know nobody, to film a movie, music video or commercial, you have to give appearances at parties, get-togethers on the set, radio station appearances or interviews, tv station appearances or interviews, appearance on talk shows, malls or clubs just to get people to see you, to sell your record, movie, book deal or because of you becoming a star. You can lose that husband or man in your life for not having enough time to spend with them because your life has changed drastically overnight into stardom. Now you're rich and famous with that big fat bank account. You dreamed all of your life being like this when you were a little child. Now your dream has come true. It could have led you on that path of loneliness or feeling empty inside because of the limited time for the ones you love; hoping that loved one can adapt or make that change to his/her lifestyle. Because in the end it could lead to divorce or separation, the profession of becoming an actor can be overwhelming. Now you can buy that big house with a spiral staircase, four bedrooms, Jacuzzi, bathtub, two and half baths and three car garage with a toy poodle but no one to share it with. Just lights, cameras, action and lines to remember. You've blown up homey. Now you can't go anywhere without someone evading your privacy with snapshots. Actors have to go everywhere with their bodyguards; becoming a prisoner in their own surroundings. They used to have their own freedom to do whatever they please; like go anywhere without anyone recognizing who they were. The actor's life becomes closed in like mom used to do, sheltering you in your own room or home. Let's look at an actor in another way. All your dreams have come true and you are living life to the fullest. You have so much money; you don't even know what to do with it. You accomplish so many things, won so many awards, even broke many barriers, achieved and accomplished a great deal that you never even could imagine doing. Now your status has diminished a little, you are seen less and less, maybe won one or two awards or none, now attention is focused on another new superstar coming to the limelight. The actor has to adapt to no attention, less shows, no awards; now that actor may fade away for a year or three because of not being in the spot light. Many actors may act out. Sometimes some actors act out because of not being in the spotlight like they used to be. The actor could act out at adult movies store, have sex or molest kids, see porno movies or be in them, become playboy's next pinup girl or guy, dance nude, go to bars get drunk or start a fight, drive fast in a Ferrari or Hummer just to get stopped by a policemen for just a little publicity, even become an abuser by beating up your spouse or girlfriend or just have groupie love or just start talking in public how bad your parents raised you or hating on your baby mama and not let us forget about drugs, get on drugs to hide what you're feeling on in the inside not able to cope with whatever problem you have. These are just some of the things that can happen to an actor once they turn big and become lonely. When you're lonely you can act out and not even be aware of it. By being an actor/actress, have you often sometimes wonder whether or not your friends come around for what you have to offer them and not for your true friendship once you become rich and famous even though they been around you when you had nothing? Being an actor when you travel around the world going to different cities and state to state, just pick up a book to read or just think about a memory of your beau or children close in your mind when traveling without your loved one. This is more of keeping things on a more positive note. Being an actor, emptiness and loneliness could creep in and the actor may not even be aware of it. Pick up a good book to read as mentioned above, listen to music, take up a play, opera or movie or a comedy show when you are away from home. Being an actor/actress, it's hard on you and the family or just being single. Always do positive and wholesome things in your life that's pleasing to others because there's always someone out there that's idolizing you or looking up to you. Your example must be kept up because of onlookers; what you do in your life and how you handle different situations your fans are looking and keeping up with you from day to day and will try to follow in your footsteps. Keep it positive because someone else will strive to keep working at their dream in becoming an actor/actress. Do all the positive things that an actor/actress can do to not steer some fan in the wrong direction.

FOSTER/ADOPTIVE PARENT

The house is empty, just you and your husband or just you by yourself. There could be a couple of dogs or cats since the kids are gone. If you're married, it might be too quiet in the house. You and your spouse might argue over everything; getting on one another nerves until its sickening. So what you may decide to do is to become a foster parent or adoptive parent. This could happen because you're lonely in your own house—too quiet. You give some thought about more children in the household beside yourselves. You also gave some thought to the fact that you raised your own kids to the best of your ability by making sure they had the best that you could afford; working day and night until they were grown and finished school. You and your spouse have just retired from your jobs. Because both of you were good parents in raising your kids you want to give someone else that chance; maybe to have a better chance at life. You could have traveled the world, didn't have to cook everyday and started painting, sewing, just relaxing, shopping until you drop or remodeled your house. But you decided to bring maybe neglected, abused, abandoned kids into your home. Now you reprise the role of motherhood/fatherhood because you're lonely for some kiddos. Being parents is great but being foster and adoptive parents is good. It shows that you have a good heart by taking in somebody else's child. Sometimes it could be a struggle and other times it could be worth it. It just depends on the child you take in. Doing this can be worth it in the long run; helping someone that needs help and guidance. If you think about it deeply, you realize these kids have felt that they are all alone in this world with no one to care about them, nobody to love them, hold them at night or hold them to just read them a bedtime story and reassure them everything is going to be okay. By letting them know that you're here to protect them and letting them know everything is going to be alright, it helps their souls inside in time to be in comfort and not scared or having a nervous stomach of being in the wrong home where harm could come to them. Sometimes once you get these kids it may not be what you thought. You could have gotten a problem child. A problem child that lies, steal, start fights at school or the class clown, hateful and mean and one that makes bad grades all the time. You, as a foster/adoptive parent, won't be lonely now because you have to give this child hope and get this child self-esteem back; which will enable this child to become a better person. It also takes patience, love, kindness, being mild-tempered and having a listening ear that can bring these kids around. Some kids you get are just perfect and smart that comes from child services and adoption agencies. Being a foster/adoptive parent says a lot about you as an individual. That's a big responsibility you're taking all over again. One thing about this is that you will be giving a child a second chance at life to become a doctor, lawyer, nurse, social worker, judge, senator, owner of their own business, inventor or be the next president of the United States. Keep in mind not every foster/adoptive parent is cut out for this because some lonely people may want to get kids just to continue that vicious cycle of physical/sexual abuse. Their loneliness can be derived from this. Sometimes the child protective services and adoption agencies forget to go back and check on these kids, regardless if they're living in a fine place/house better than where they were at. What's on the inside of a material house doesn't make a person good or mean that child is safe. To make a long story short, because a house is gorgeous in the inside doesn't make that person's heart good. Sometimes some foster/adoptive parents can scare a child to death by saying if you tell what I've done to you they just put you in another home and that the same thing will happen to you over again; putting fear in that child making them so afraid of you that they won't tell. Their grades start slipping but you or nobody won't recognize these signs. Poor kids, they may feel that now the system went down the drain; forgot to ask them if they're okay here at this house once they're adoptive. Please somebody check on me; the abusive adoptive child replies. I may have got off a little bit here. I wanted to give a little input, to a child lost in the system, that could bring that child into a world of loneliness especially when a child tells a person how someone else is mistreating them but no one believes them or no one pays any attention to the signs of an abuse child that's done by the foster/adoptive parent. They crawl into their own world which is stopped. That means they stop talking, thinking, believing in them, stop eating and always have their head down—low, low self-esteem loneliness here brings about a desertion feeling. The system abandons them since they're adoptive. Keeping foster or adopting kids is a good thing. It shows that you are a unique and extraordinary individual. Then whenever your maker calls you, you can rest in peace and have God's grace because you went out of your way for someone else's child you didn't even know. That individual you helped will always be grateful and appreciative to you for what you've done for them even though they may not show it like you want them too. When they become grown you will see the end result. You will see their successfulness, happiness within them and completeness in their lives. This will make you happy for what you did for them.

ELDERLY (AN ALZHEIMER'S PERSON)

An elderly person is sitting at home in her rocking chair rocking away, living all alone in an empty house. The kids are grown; now living their own lives, caught up in their own world. They have forgotten about mom or dad at home alone; just caught up in their everyday life of surviving in this world from day to day. Now the elderly person has retired from their job where they put in anywhere from fifteen to thirty-five years of service. Now the elderly hear no more sounds of laughter or noise in the house, no TV playing, no music playing; just quietness that surrounds the house. So what happens is, as you may know the elderly person becomes lonely. Guess right. Being by oneself, the elderly or someone advanced in age may tend to start talking to themselves and even answering themselves back. The elderly person may become heavily involved in church and church activities in hope of finding friends to come and visit them. This is still not enough to heal the void in ones life. When church is over, the elderly person goes home to an empty house once again. But emptiness ends up captivating oneself. So the elderly person starts giving large sums of money to the church for recognition and attention from friends; for someone to come and visit them. Not only that, salespeople stop by or call on the telephone. The elderly are easy to influence in being swindled out of their money. Starving for company, this may cause the elderly to invite people that they don't even know to their home even the neighbor they may have never liked but they coming around now. These type of friends may have one thing in mind; it's dollar signs. All about that Benjamins because they know the elderly have the money. The elderly person is just thinking of having a friend to check on them from time to time because their children don't come around to check on them anymore.

Even carrying on a real conversation with them makes them feel good inside. Some friends in the church and neighbors can take advantage of the elderly because they have no one to come and check on them. The elderly may not realize that they can become prey to some people they think are good at heart. Sometimes we need to watch out for people like these if we really care about the elderly. The elderly's children need to keep up with their mom or dad because the elderly can be used by others for greed. If the children don't keep up with their parents, they can give away their whole life saving or earnings just because nobody's around to see about them. When money is gone, friends are gone. The friends that the elderly person had either died or moved away. So, what do the elderly do now? They probably crawl into their little shell; back to talking to themselves, washing the dishes, cleaning the house, cooking for oneself. After a while, the elderly minds begin to slip because they're in a house all by themselves—no one to see about them. That's when Alzheimer's may come into play. One thing we need to keep in mind is that Alzheimer's is defined as this: forgetfulness and remembers the past clearly but can't remember yesterday or today minutes and seconds ago. It's also hard for them to remember the mates they might have been with for fifty years. Being forgetful can cause loneliness with the elderly. The elderly mind begins to shutdown with this illness. We need to always show love to them; keeping a daily watch on them so they won't become lonely in their old age when they're seventy or eighty years old. Because they mind may slip when they are at home by themselves. If you are keeping an eye on the elderly, you can notice their house for instance, when were the dishes last washed? Are the dishes clean? Are their broken plates on the floor? Is the house clean? Is the floor vacuumed? Did they try to cook and burn their food to eat or leave the stove on? Did they wash their clothes? Are the clothes clean or they still dirty? Never leave the elderly in the house by themselves but move them in with you, not a nursing home or a retirement facility because you don't have the time or don't want to give up your life for them but keep in mind that they raised you and gave up their lives for you so you can have a better future. Being home with their children, hearing baby noise or hearing children talking makes the world of difference. This will indeed keep them young at heart. Stop them from not remembering. I really believe this is the best medicine for the elderly; just being in touch with the family life consisting of mom, dad, son, daughters, nieces or nephews or grandchildren. This disease could be a thing of the past if it's caught in time. To me an Alzheimer's patient is a person that lets loneliness slip into their minds, causing them not to deal with yesterday or today but always remembering everything in their past not the present; like blocking certain things out or parts of their mind shuts down. Never leave an elderly person alone in a house no more than three months because they could feel that nobody cares about them. Always watch after your parents that become the elderly so that this disease doesn't sneak up on them and take their minds away from them. Being loved and shown love is what the elderly need. When the elderly have someone or somebodies in their company, their minds don't slip back or forgetfulness doesn't settle in. But the elderly person stays up to date with current events that are taking place in their lives, if people are around them. Be good children, you just might store good deeds in heaven by watching over the elderly until the maker calls them home. You won't have any regrets that would eat you up inside for what you should have done.

MARRIED PERSON

A married person can really be associated with loneliness. Let's discuss this in some ways. For instance, you get married to a loved one. You go on that bum of a honeymoon trip you always desired and dreamed of every since you was a little child. You might even travel to Bahamas, Aruba, Jamaica, Hawaii, St. Thomas or the Virgin Islands. While you're on that delightful honeymoon, you and your loved mate may make passionate love sun up to sun down. Once your honeymoon is over you come home and face the real world. Hey, the honeymoon is over. Now you go back to your daily routine which could include visiting in-laws where the mother-in-law prepares dinner every Sunday after church; then you might go visit your spouse friends which could includes dancing, barbecuing, playing cards, watching movies, going clubbing, going to friends parties, going to get-togethers, going out to eat every other night or day, going to family weddings and to the movies on the weekend. This is something that's done with your mate in your first to five years of marriage. Then one day everything that you and your mate used to do slows down. You really begin to get to know one another better than you thought you knew when you dated him/her. You get to know what he/she really likes or doesn't like, what that person may tolerate or not tolerate, what his/her limitations are, how he/she really is as a person, how that mate may feel about children, life insurance policies or themselves, who he/she might put before you or who comes first to him/her, how that person keeps the house, how that person spends money, do the bills get paid, do his/her children comes before you, is he/she out with his/her friends every weekend or during the weekdays. Once you know the answers to these questions you know your mate. Since you're a married couple and all and everything is on a routine basis, you become more settled and comfortable in your marriage with your spouse. You might even gain weight because you just know he/she is the one and only you will ever be with and you're confident that he/she will never leave you. Then you start letting yourself go because you come to think that he/she will accept you as you are since you're married now. Even if you had a bad attitude or was a wife beater, oversexed person, just mean and never smile, cheater, Bible based man/woman, drunk, arguer, workaholic, sweet as you can be, child abuser or just a selfish person or a nagger. Then boom! Your mate starts to act funny with you like he might even hate he married you or vice versa. Then one day you come home. Your mate out of the blue moves out of your bedroom; no warning signs you could have detected. Just up and done it. Forcing both of you to be in separate rooms and the communications stop, then loneliness steps in the room—no one to talk to but the walls. What marriage leaves you empty inside and lonely? You try to figure out what or where you went wrong. What did you do? Then your mind starts thinking how you both used to talk everyday about everything that went on between you; went to church together, shared everything together the good and the bad, went out to eat together, done everything together as husband and wife. Then everything stops, gradually or suddenly. Even your sexual life comes to a halt. Would you ever have thought you could be married and lonely? Once sensible persons come to their senses they says something like this, do we have a problem in our marriage? Let's talk about it but the spouse says no. As the day and night passes by, the spouse may get up and leave. You become lonely and sad in an empty house all by yourself. The other mate may not come home until late at night; making you feel hurt inside because of all you gave into your marriage. The house becomes so quiet; like when you were single. Now, that's an empty feeling, whether a spouse admits it or not. When that spouse does comes home you probably are asleep or playing asleep. Then the next day, that spouse may begin doing things separately from you; not including you anymore. So you began to drift apart; doing things alone but if you probably knew this would happen you probably would never have gotten married in the first place. In reality, this is how some marriages are. You have to learn to cope even when time gets rough, even if you are lonely. Don't divorce or separate; where you both are not in the same house.

Just endure, in time, situations always gets better and can bring about a change. Keep prayer and God in your marriage. Never close the door on the memorable things you did together. Try to rekindle the flame even though it maybe hard. When your spouse comes in, give him/her kisses and hugs even though he/she may not want them and even shrugs you away which turn his/her head. This will make him cheery eventually. He/she may not show it right then but a person contemplating marriage for the simple reason that a person is tired of being alone, decides to get married and not for love. This is something that happens very often in life when you're lonely. Never stopping to think about an important decision in life; to make or just doing it because your close friend is getting married. Making a decision like this could be disastrous if the marriage doesn't last or work. Be very careful about decision/choices you make in life due to loneliness because you could end up regretting it for the rest of your life. You could lose your life in some marriages that are done for the wrong reason especially when you might want to end it. Marriage is something you take seriously because this person is the one whom you will be spending the rest of your like with forever. Then no loneliness will creep in for sure. One last thing in our marriages or being a married person by yourself, you have to be satisfied with your mate; remembering that just about every man/woman has issues. There's no perfect marriage. You have to learn how to deal with issues and problems with the help of the good lord above. Become satisfied with that mate in the marriage arrangement. If you were single again, you would be complaining about being lonely because you don't have a man or woman in your life. You want one so bad. Enjoy who you are with and another thing, when we spend a lifetime in our marriage giving it everything we have. You spent anywhere from five to fifteen or fifty years with this mate; been through hell and back or through hell and high waters or through thick and thin. Then don't let a younger woman/man come along in your life and ruin your marriage; maybe giving you your youth back that you may thought you have lost, you think you might be in love with that person and the sex is better than the mate you were married too for fifteen to fifty years. Then one day, you could wake up feeling regret that you made a mistake and should have stayed married or faithful to the one that you spent so many years with. It could have been the fact that you could have been going through the change of life or wanted to feel young again. You, as married people, need to get back to being with a mate for fifteen to fifty years; going the long haul. No matter what! Remember that staying and running that race with our mates no matter what you may have to go through with that person because God can step in at anytime and change anything within that person to become a better mate if you believe and have faith in the lord. That's all it takes.

SEX

Enjoyment of sex is great when you reach your orgasm. Having a mate to touch you in special places of your body is enjoyment; sucking of the tiddies, playing with your vagina or penis, taking syrup, jelly or whip cream placing on lower parts of your body and someone licking it up. It feels good; put you in a trance like being in never ever world. Concentrating on the enjoyment of sex is another part of loneliness because you can miss it when you're not able to get it. Your mood swings; changes making you very bitchy or moody. Some of you are used to getting sex on a daily basis or maybe sex has stopped completely or you might be getting it once or twice a week. That would really blow your mind. Sex is a form of lovemaking that result in feelings coming from the inside of your heart releasing pressure of love or body heat. When you don't get it, you think of ways of how to get the sex. You may even dream of having it constantly and even touching yourself and getting yourself off when you don't have a person around to release the pressure that's built up inside of you. The real world has done this. You know who you are. Sex is also what your body craves for when you don't get it. You never stop thinking of it until you get it. Your inner feelings become empty and sad because you no longer have that comfort of a man/women next to you. You have to learn to move on and if you get a man/woman, learn to get to know him/her first before you have sex with that person. Make sure that person gets tested for AIDS/HIV and hepatitis C so you won't be scared for life or die. This may be hard for some of you because if we ask them to do this we could lose that person before it even gets started and boom you maybe by yourself again. But if that person is not in agreement to getting this done, that person is not meant for you in the first place. Safe sex is the best sex;

than taking death by the hand. This way you can live continuously and have great sex when it becomes available to you. Always think about who you might have sex with carefully so you won't be doing it with someone you don't care about or love. Make sure you get back to the basics of loving someone that you are going to marry. We could pay the price of living or dying and that choice would be yours. Sex could also be a mind-boggling thing. If you're thinking about it day and night, we grew up in a society where everyone is having sex. Sex can be a fragile thing, just like breaking a glass if you drop it. It breaks. Sex can break your heart especially if you are in love with that person and that person leaves you. Think about this. When you're craving for sex, you can't get it. Your body just starts craving and tingling all below for that magic stick/pernana each and everyday. Because of all the diseases out there you have to restrain yourself and practice self control and safe sex. There's nothing wrong with having your sex toys to fulfill your sexual desires so you can stay away from AIDS and be disease free. You do get lonely for that companionship. Hopefully you don't get that feeling of craving for sex and go out there and have sex with someone you just met or don't even know and not use protection. Waking up scared for life with AIDS, herpes, chlamydia or HIV is frightening. This can happen with one night of pleasure just to fulfill a sexual need. Ask yourself was it worth it? Did you awaken yourself to the world of the unknown AIDS? That's the consequence of sex without protection or a marriage mate if that mate is unfaithful to the person they love. This is what loneliness can cause you to do. Sex is something everyone wants in their life sometime or another but it may not be healthy for you. In life today, there's a need for the comfort of man/woman. But whatever we do for sex think about our decision to have sex carefully. Ask the important question before having sex. Is that person disease free? Will I marry that person? Is my relationship with that person based solely on sex? Am I having sex because I'm lonely and scared to be by myself? Do I really know the person I'm having sex with? What's God viewpoint in the Bible on sex?

ISOLATION

Isolation is a deep topic that loneliness can be associated with. Isolation could make you feel like you're always misunderstood by people; causing you to be forced in a corner not relating to anyone because everything you say or do get twisted around some kind of way. Someone tells you something that happened in the family. A deep dark family secret, you go tell someone else because you might not be able to hold hot water. It's like you said it but in reality someone told it to you because they could be tired of holding that secret in. They know without a doubt that you will be the one to spread it but they don't want to talk about it or tell someone on their own. But you're made out to be the bad guy. But nobody might believe that you didn't say it. If you really think about it, you would have not known if someone didn't tell you. Then you're labeled as messy causing you to be by yourself or isolate yourself again or crawl up in a little corner all by yourself. Isolation can also be thought of as not choosing to associate yourself with others; maybe due to the fear of not being liked by others and not being able to communicate or not being around anybody. You're usually a person that goes to work and back home. People make you uncomfortable. Being around them, you're just not at ease. When you go places, people freak you out when they look at you. When they walk behind you or pass you by on each side, you just get paranoid and want to run back home and get in your house and never come out again. Some people just panic in the world today when they began to mingle, such as going to the mall walking to catch a bus or at a bus station or at the airport and going to eat in restaurants which this is a daily way of life. Because you're thinking of one way doing it alone, now self-improvement is another form of isolation. Think about it; if you live in the ghetto, you get rich or famous or make enough money on your job to leave. Will you leave your type of environment or would you stay? That's when fear starts up because you isolate yourself to your surrounding. For instance, when a person stay stuck in the house fear of eyes watching them can be related to loneliness. Have you ever thought about why a person would crawl to a corner sit down with their hands over their head and feet crossed over together Indian style? When you isolate yourself in corner, you put your mind in bondage; locking out all your emotions inside of you; just in that depressed mode or state of mind; excluding everyone from you; maybe thinking that your life could have taken a wrong turn somewhere. You try to figure out how you can correct the situation or how to move on with yourself; no one to ask you how you're doing, what you're doing today; no one to visit you or knock at the door. Everything is simply empty causing you to withdraw from anything in your house because most likely you could be playing your TV, listening to the radio, cleaning up your house, taking a bubble bath or shower. But you chose to be in that corner of doom. Isolation is really related to fear around or inside of you where loneliness creeps in. You should always have someone surrounding you with love; maybe lending a listening ear, keeping your head up, your self esteem in yourself. Keep your mind and views open in everyday life problems. When a different situation comes up; when you just can't cope; get the good book out and pray to the good lord to help you so you won't close yourself in. Remember you, the person/individual, hold the key to your daily life problems, surroundings, peace of mind and your ability to cope with dilemmas in life. Always keep the faith and everything will be alright. Let people in because the fear will go away and loneliness won't creep in.

INCARCERATION

Guess what, I got locked up today doing something stupid. It could have been a number of things like breaking into someone house, robbing a store, raping a child, woman or man, shooting or killing someone, beating up your loved one or a friend, writing a hot check, selling drugs or just being an con artist. These are just some things that can land you behind bars. Now you're in a cell all alone by yourself or with another criminal; no family member, no girlfriend, nor your best friend, nor can you just get up and go visit anybody because you're locked up. Your freedom on the outside has been taken away from you because of the criminal act you committed. Sometimes we never think about how easy we had it until our rights are taken away from us. Now our phone conversations are also limited because there are other people that have to talk on the phone besides you. You have to wait until it's your turn to use the phone. As each day goes by we get lonely for the people that are close to us. Now you have to think about how to survive being incarcerated, a world unknown to you behind bars for the criminal acts committed. Now you have to find your place or find what to do in prison to pass the time away. Now it's your first night in a cell all by yourself. As you lay down on a nasty, pissy smelling mattress looking at the ceiling up there thinking about where you went wrong in your life or you may not have done nothing; just railroaded. Then you look around and realize you have one toilet and another bed to share—a room with someone else. Being incarcerated helps you to realize that you are isolated from the world outside. You are alone. Then reality hits you. You may even ask yourself; how do I cope with my surroundings? Will these other inmates take my manhood/womanhood? Who do I call on now? I'm incarcerated. Had I not done all those bad things on the outside which could include being in a gang and doing acts that expected of me from my gang leader, breaking in people houses, selling drugs, stealing cars, stereos and holding up a grocery or convenience stores for money. Ask yourself was it all worth it? Do you have anything that you can show for what you did when you committed that crime for the time spent being locked up? If not, then it was not worth it at all especially if you get caught and the police get what you stole back or the person you try to kill didn't die or run con games on people you come in contact with thinking that its just the right thing to do at that particular time because you think they are stupid. Then you ask yourself why you took your own freedom for granted. What if you decided to take a rap for your homey and you didn't even commit the crime for which you were convicted for? Was this a smart move on your part? If you actually think about it, that person is out on the outside in the real world. You're stuck in prison while that person or homey has gone on with his/her life; forgot about you. You're by your lonesome self. Then you say in your sleep looking up at the ceiling that my own homey has forgot about me in here. I took the rap for nothing. I'm alone my freedom has been taken away and nobody cares about me. Locked up and confused, that's what incarceration gets you to feel inside. Being alone in a cell makes you also think about some things in your life you could have done right but (oh no) the devil made you do those wrong criminal acts that you had in your heart; to do that lead you to be locked up in a cell all alone. One thing I can say when you are incarcerated the first thing you think about is a relationship with God. How bad you hurt mom, dad or both parents, wife or husband or how you let yourself down or your children down. Even after you get incarcerated you will always reflect on the fact that whoever you were around always told you what path you were headed down. You just didn't want to stop what you were doing or listen to them because you knew it all. Now sometimes being incarcerated may help you to get on that straight and narrow road; to help straighten your behavior out and make the right decisions in your life that you can benefit from such as getting an education like a high school diploma, GED or a college degree; something you could have gotten on the outside if you did the right thing from the start. It took being incarcerated to get your mind to click the right way. Now you probably start going to church;

something you should have been doing from the start which probably would have helped you but wait a minute. You wouldn't have gotten into the type of criminal act committed by you if you gone to church because you would have reformed your mind as to how the lord would feel if you did this or that. You may not have landed in jail or prison today. So basically you're reforming yourself to becoming a nice person with good thoughts. The type of person you could have been all along. This is what you do when you have all this time on your hands being incarcerated; because you have so much time until you get out. Being locked up, you really miss your friends and loved ones; missing them may even make you cry many nights; even your heart can began to hurt inside due to emptiness or loneliness inside; even longing to be on the outside but you know this may not happen now due to the road you went down or took in your life. You cannot even go back and correct it. Being incarcerated, time and loneliness go hand in hand. It's funny, someone that had it all ends up here. You know the old saying if I could go back, do it all over again and change the time I would have. But be realistic because you can't. But know now you have to cope with your actions and make a new family in there. Now you close your eyes you began to think in your mind saying you should have went to church, kept God in your life on a daily basis; what if I would have done this or what if I would have done that. What if's come into play. Your mind is thinking; you should have been really listening to your parents, grandmother, brother or sister, aunt or uncle when they tried to tell you what road or path you were headed in. You couldn't see for the fun you were having and the wrong you were doing in your life; thinking it would never come to an end or you're to clever to get caught. You had so many wrong types of friends that you followed, knowing your inner conscience told you to stop before you would get caught for doing bad acts. Shoulda, wouldda and couldda are the things you should have asked yourself before committing crimes in the world outside instead of being incarcerated in a cell in the inside. You tell yourself that you long for your freedom but you took it for granted. Then you say crying to yourself; thinking to yourself i'm lonely for my wife or girlfriend, family, friends and my children. Oh I let them down.

Then when you receive visitors from the real world on the outside, you tell them to please forgive me and don't end up where I am. Keep the Bible and God in your life. Listen to those that give you wisdom and share life experiences with you so you won't choose the wrong path. If you don't know God just get on your knees and pray. Tell God what's on your mind. Talk to him like you talk to your buddy and end the prayer "in Jesus' name" amen.

WORKAHOLIC

Workaholism could be a form of loneliness in getting away from one's situation. When you wake up every morning to get up and go to work. We work seven and a half hours or eight hours a day in a normal work period instead of going home when the work day ends. You stay and work overtime continuously. Guess what? You do have a family at home that's waiting on you. But instead of you going home you would rather work an additional two to five hours over; depriving your family of your time and attention with them at home. Just maybe you could be running away from a problem that has developed at the house. There maybe some kind of void deep inside of you that has you not coming home from work. You working on that job staying late to run away from some problem you might have. No doubt, you probably don't want to talk about it either. When there's a void inside of you, you share not to talk about the problem but pour your heart out into your work. This is a form of loneliness. When you're at work, working away; it's lonely there. If you are the only one there, you just concentrate on that job working away in an office all alone; no one to talk to but your phone on the desk, if you pick it up. Maybe your radio is turned on or you just start talking to yourself. A lot of times we say we're working on that job to catch up on a bill, trying to save money or trying to help a loved one get out of debt or yourself out of debt. Is this just an excuse we come up with to hide what's actually bothering us? But actually there may not be anything at home to come to. That's loneliness too. Perhaps you're a single person; you have no one to come home too. So what you may do is work late; working and working until you exhaust yourself. Because being home is too alone. When you make it home, all you can do is take a bath and go straight to bed. Then the next morning comes quickly, time to get up and go to work again, same old routine, rise and shine. Then you work on weekends, never having a day to yourself or enjoying you. Seven days a week working back to back sun up until sun down. You have to be running from something. You may not be aware of it. Instead of spending time at home relaxing and enjoying your house you'd rather be at work. Something is wrong with that picture. Sometimes we need to be aware because in life you only live once. If you're married and have a family, you need to be home to enjoy your life there with your husband/wife and kids; those are precious moments and memories that you can never get back if you miss any of them. If you're single, there's a lot you can do for yourself if you're not working late. For instance; going to movies, dining out in restaurants, traveling, exercising, reading a book, dancing, boating, swimming, bowling, going to the mall shopping, church, calling a friend over or talking on the telephone or cell phone, playing video games, singles meetings at church socials to find a date or mate and playing board games also. This will fill that void in your life that's there. Self-consciously, you may not be aware of your issues inside of you. On these jobs, being a workaholic is running away once again from whatever issue or problem you may have. You may be working because you think you may get a promotion but the person that does the least work on these jobs today is the one that gets the promotion; sometimes a younger person. What if working so much causes you to have a heart attack and you passed away or what if someone broke into the office and raped or beat you up or set fire to the building at work. Then you would have had flashbacks as to what you should have done in your life before something terrible like this happens to you. All your job is going to do, if you pass or if you get injured somehow, is just hire and find someone else to replace you. Then you will be only a memory to them until everyone has forgotten about you in the office. Never let that void come up inside of you; where it has you working all the time and forgetting about you, the person or your family. Even though these jobs want you to wear four to five different hats, never getting paid for what you're worth but that's the life in the job market. You'd be trying to keep up with the workflow on your desk because you need a job to pay your bills. At the same time, your salary never increases; just staying the same but bringing on more stress in your life. Never get that kind of void or loneliness in your life but always recognize it and deal with whatever problem that may come up with you in your life. Life is too short not to enjoy our home life or family life. Remember you can be here today and gone tomorrow. Life is never promised to anyone. So enjoy your life while you can because we do two things in life, that's live and die which we have no control over. So you don't want to be working too hard driving yourself in the ground and no good for nobody. But whatever you feeling inside work it out with your husband/wife or with yourself maybe even praying about it or reading the bible or calling a close friend to talk to. Enjoy your life and you as an individual because God gave life as a precious gift to you to enjoy; not to be a workaholic. That's not good for anybody or the soul. See God knows your needs and desires in your life before you even come to him in prayer. You got to ask him for what you need and he will grant them to you accordingly. He is a God that's right on time.

DRUG ADDICTION/ALCOHOLIC

Drug addiction is a narcotic substance that controls the mind, body and soul. An alcoholic is a person that hides in a bottle. Just how is these associated with loneliness; when a person is on drugs they take these due to problems, they just can't cope with but deep down inside they're emotionally disturbed. When a person turns to drugs, they're just running from something they do not want to deal with just like a alcoholic. Take this for instance; this is a true story of a person I became acquainted with. She became a crack addict because she always wanted her mother's love. Her mother had her pick of her children. She had three kids, the only ones she loved the most was the middle child and her only son. She never showed the oldest any love at all like the other kids. She basically was never there for any of her children—let the truth be told. She didn't know this. The oldest daughter was never shown love by her mother; probably she might have turned out different with the course of her life but by not having her mother's love she acted out. For instance, running away from home all the time, skipping school and sleeping with every man she came in contact with even if it was her family members. She just lost her dignity within her. Basically she became emotionally and mentally disturbed within. This is also associated with loneliness when she became grown and had children of her own. How you were raised is how you will raise your children unless you can break the vicious cycle. She probably didn't show them love like her mom didn't show her. A mother should show her kids love because it makes a big of difference growing up. When she became grown and finished school, she did make it happen for herself. She had everything, such as being a very well dressed woman always wearing designer clothes, had good jobs making fifty grand or better, children dressed like her, she had a new car every year, fine furniture, plenty of friends in high places, party all the time, put family members through school and paid family bills if they got behind. She looked like a model; beautiful woman; had everything going for herself; could get any man she wanted. But doing this all she must have broken down at one point in her life. One thing you have to do is get help from a doctor that you can talk to about what had happened to you in your childhood life. Nobody noticed her, her mother was always entertaining her friends. All her kids never really saw their mother much or their mother wasn't there if they needed her. Her oldest daughter started turning to her friends. One day she was up and the next day she was down overnight. Then she started hanging with a wrong relative that introduce her to crack; one of the reasons she got on drugs was her loneliness for love from her mother and the fact that her stepfather sexually abused her. Her mother knew it was happening and allowed this to go on with her daughter. This made her not love herself because she felt like love wasn't shown to her as she was growing up. When love is not shown to you, love can affect the whole outcome of your life. You go into a world of darkness keeping everything locked up inside of you; not talking about what was bothering you as a child but thinking that once you are grown you can cope with what went wrong in your life and make changes in your life. But at the end the good thing, she recognized this was the reason for her drug addiction. But her problem lied deep within her soul which had caused her to withdraw from her surroundings which brought about loneliness. She would always say she's not in the real world but lived in a drug world. Let me be alone and deal with my own demons. That's exactly what you're dealing with; it's the demons inside of you. Doing drugs she was in and out of maybe twenty rehabilitation centers or more but always saying she can stop for good when she wanted to. But never did because once she came home for about three to four hours that craving called her back or in other words that devil was riding her back. Drug addiction can be kicked if you, the individual, want to stop. No one can do that for you but you and the good lord. All you have to do is pray because God is a hearer of prayers. God searches the heart. If you have a sincere heart, you can kick this habit. He sees if you're for real or not. It doesn't matter how many rehabilitation centers you go to. They won't do you any good or help you until you make up your mind, change your association and pray to the lord for help because you've come to a point in your life that you do not want to continue living like this and doing drugs. Drug addiction can be kicked if you, the individual, want to stop; no one can make that decision for you but you. Not even moving to another city, state or neighborhood because a drug addict will find that drug somehow no matter what. Never underestimate what a crackhead won't do for drugs. Don't fool yourself. Believe this! Doing drugs is a mind thing. If you think about doing drugs all the time especially if you're in a rehabilitation place day in and day out trying to kick the habit. When you get out you go right back to doing those drugs over and over again because it's in your mind. You are always thinking about doing those drugs in your mind. If you don't think about doing drugs in your mind you won't do them. Sometimes you have to get on your knees and ask God for help through prayer everyday. All the rehabilitation centers that you are in and out of, if God is not present in you trying to quit the habit, your effects will fail. Not only that, you also have to stop on your own; by yourself. You have to want to do this not just talking about what you gonna do but do it. Stop selling your soul to the crack house or streets. Get clean and stay clean. Drug addiction ties in with an alcoholic. Being an alcoholic is a drug addiction in itself. An alcoholic become their true self when they are drinking. That bottle helps an alcoholic to be brave and fearless or cope with problems or situations that they couldn't deal with while being sober. Three words that are associated with an alcoholic are brave/cope/not sober or BCNS. Some alcoholics come home drunk every payday; Friday night fight specials or every weekend breaking up everything in the house; may even beat up anyone who gets in that alcoholic person way. Then once that alcoholic person become sober, he/she doesn't remember a thing he/she may have done that day or before. Then he/she may want to apologize for their wrongdoings not remembering they were drunk and acted a fool. Then for two to three days, he/she may stay isolated in their room all by themselves because they are embarrassed about what they have done. But once payday comes around again and Friday is here. Look out for Dr. Jekyll and Mr./Miss Hyde, it would happen all over again. When a person stays in their room and secludes themselves from everyone that is loneliness. They have issues they don't want to deal with. This person has always been probably a quiet person until payday comes and its freaky Friday. They turn into a whole other person; like a person turning into a werewolf when a full moon appears. Look out! How many people get devoured tonight? An alcoholic hides behind a bottle; afraid to cope with what's bothering them; wishing they were this way and that way but they're not. When you think about it, older people have always said that a drunk person always speaks the truth when they drink or get drunk causing them to act out of their normal self if they were sober. My perception of drug addicts and alcoholics is that they're running away from problems in their life and not being brave enough to cope and stay sober to deal with. One more thing, in order to kick any habits you have, get out of the surroundings that you are in or bad association. Remember bad association spoils useful habits that are good. Be around people that can uplift you with encouraging words and accept their help when they offer it to you. Definitely stop being around people that lead you to crack houses and give you crack free because they need a partner to help do it with them; tell you lies if you do it with them you won't get hooked—because you will. They just want you to still be like them. Stop drinking that bottle and doing drugs, going to bars, beer joints or tiddies bars until you are drunk and don't know who you are. Which makes you turn into an alcoholic/drug addict but be BCS brave/cope/ and sober and that will get you where you need to be in life with yourself so you will have no regrets. Don't go through life thinking you have to make up for every mistake you made in your life. Don't let your brain eat you up inside and out for not doing the right thing. You can still have your full senses, your capabilities of thinking for yourself making good decisions that will cause you to live your life without regrets. If you make a mistake and you're trying to keep bad habits just pick yourself up if you can and move forward, don't look back and don't live in the past. Keep striving forward because a change within you will come eventually. Don't give up on you.

DATING GAME

When you become single and have to start dating all over again with different people, it's called the dating game. The dating game can become lonely in the sense of a person being by oneself when no one is in that person's life. The dating game gets off and running with dating different people. You can find a person to date at a newspaper stand, newspaper advertisement, the internet, movies, grocery store, church, on the freeway, calling the wrong number, through a friend, the mall, radio stations, cruises, clubs, restaurants, workplace, school, doctor's office, airport, plays, operas, standing or waiting for a bus, sport games or bars, billiards, bowling alley, parks and concerts. Keep in mind before I go into details on some dating episodes when you date you're looking basically for a companion or friend; something that will lead to a true relationship. Everybody wants a wholesome relationship; someone that's not on drugs, an alcoholic, or an abuser—both physically and verbally. You can meet some good people that are: wholesome and intellectual, that have something going for themselves, career-oriented, that want to make a relationship work, keep a clean house, good cook or teach them to be a cook, good lovers or you can teach them to be good lovers, church-going persons that are not pretending to be until he/she makes that catch, a person that won't have everybody up in all your business; for instance people on the outside telling you what to do and how to handle your problems and situations that you could be faced with which they did not get the information from you but your other party. You also want someone that has the same goals that you have. These are just some things a person looks into another person if they want someone in their life. They've always been a workaholic; never took the time to settle down, a person that's been scared of commitment, a person that got their degree and now they are ready to settle down, get married and have a family. Whatever the case maybe the first step is to date and that is called the dating game. When you start to date that will get you out of that lonely mode that you've probably been in so often. Dating can help develop that process of being lonely without someone or somebody to share your life with. This is what puts you into that lonely state of mind of always doing everything in your life by yourself. Loneliness effects you deep inside your soul emotionally because it eats away at you. You really can't explain it; almost. When you're by yourself deep down inside, you tell yourself that I don't need anyone, no more headaches from a relationship, free from any type of drama that a relationship brings. But in reality, you are wishing for someone to come into your life to talk to. Some women may have three types of men in their lives so they won't ever become lonely or loneliness creeps in. The first man is a sugar daddy, one that gives you money all the time and pays your bills. The second man is a Mandingo man, one that lays that pipe in you or gives you great sex that makes you reach your highest peak. The third man is a gay boy; please no one take offense, but this is someone that you just can talk about all your men/women problems or just a friend you can only talk to. Men have the same thing also but we never hear them talk about it. Now let's experience the club scene. You walk into the club checking out the men/women and trying to find a seat at the same time. You find one and he or she is on the dance floor. He/she looks good to the eyes. You are sharp as a tack from head to toe thinking that there is not a man/woman in this club you cannot have. Then the waitress comes up and asks if you would like a drink. You say yes and place your order. Then someone catches your eye like cotton candy sticking to your fingers. You try to get his attention; you even try to look at him to see if you both have that eye to eye contact. Your eyes may follow him/her to his/her seat maybe even buying him/her a drink or two. You try to get up enough nerve to ask for that person's number so you can find out what this person is all about; trying to just get that love connection going. Then you go out on a couple of dates with that person you met in a club; trying to get to know that person by talking on the phone all day and night until the wee early morning hours. Then you find out that's not what you wanted in a person; he/she may have portrayed some qualities that you may not like about him/her. Leave that person and don't feel bad about letting go. Just start dating again and again until you find the right one. Now please remember when dating you really don't find a good one in the club unless that person is one out of a million because the old saying is if you find a person in a club that's where he/she will always be. Now let's take the internet scene: you surf the internet until someone opens up a chat room or let you in, some people make a love connection there, you make plans to meet this person and you find out he/she is nothing that he/she described himself/herself to be in the internet. Once you go out with that person and have great entertainment whatever that may be, you say he/she is not for me. You end up coming home to an empty house again. But be careful on the internet because the person you're talking too may not appear to be what that person seems to be. You could be talking to a younger person, a serial killer or a pervert. Now let's go to the used-to-be boyfriend/girlfriend you had in your life. You call this person out of the blue, saying to yourself I used to date him/her. Let's see if I can make that love connection again. After going on plenty of dates with that person again and again; thinking that person may have changed since you date him/her last. Then you realize why that person was your ex. You end up letting that person go once again. Now you're by yourself once again; no one at home with you but the TV and phone. Now let me take a seat back and go to church. Some people feel they can go to church and find a date. But church should not be thought of like trying to find a date. As you attend church that Sunday, you end up checking all the ministers/pastors in the church with their fine suits on and listening to some of their fine glorified sermons. Let's not forget the deacons, trustees and assistants. You even get to the point you check out to see if the pastor has a wife; to see if he's available. Then your eyes rove about on the other women/men in the church to see if they are sitting with their husbands/wives; trying to find out who's married or single; to see if you can make a catch. It's kind of hard to distinguish when you should really be listening to the message that the pastor is bringing from the pulpit. If somebody in the church is for you, the lord will put you together with that person not you. But you distracted yourself from the message at hand. Once church is over, what do you do? You go home and you open the door to your house. You say to your lonely self is anybody home but no one to responds to you. So you turn on your TV and check your answering machine for any messages but no one called you. So the only company you have is the TV at that moment. So while you're watching TV you get in that lonely mode again. You start thinking on how you can go out on a date with someone. So you go up and at it to find someone again. Ask yourself why it is lonely in here; full of loneliness. I just have to find someone to relate to; keep my avenues or options open to find someone; keep that dating game on until you find the right somebody. Just be patient and practice a little self-control in the different steps that you take in your life when you're lonely and nobody's there for you because when you're not expecting someone to come into your life that's when someone enters; when you least expect it. You could meet anybody anywhere that you may go. Whatever the case may be someone will come eventually into your life. Make sure when you find that right person, you ask all the right questions concerning what you want out of a relationship or mate. Then that dating game is over. If the person is not for you, let him/she go right then without a doubt. If he/she is the right person and fits your description for a wife/husband, use protection until you tested for AIDS/HIV then your dating game comes to a true stop.

DECEASED LOVED ONE

When a loved one you are close to passes away, you do feel an emptiness inside; a pain that sores like a sore thumb that's seem to never go away. It hurts deep inside your soul. You never stop thinking about the person that's gone. You can't get that person out of your mind. All those fond memories stored in your brain that you remember and cherish forever. When your think of your deceased loved one, it's like they are there for real but only in spirit. You can't see them, touch them or feel them but you can talk to them. You could be anywhere, like in your car, at the gravesite, jogging, riding a bicycle, running a race, walking, skating, or at the park and you start talking to your deceased loved one telling them your problems and what's going on with everybody and what they have missed since they have passed on and can they help you if you ran into a crossroad in your life and don't know which way to turn. You may ask for help in decision making or just help to show you a way out of a situation. It's very hard when a deceased loved one is gone; sometimes you may not be able to pick yourself up if you depended on them all your life to bail you out of jams such as: give you a place to stay, help pay some bills when you come up short, buy you clothes so you won't look like a mess or you won't feel out of place if you going somewhere, keep up your appearances and keep up your hairdos and haircuts. All of the above is loneliness creeping inside of your soul that affects you emotionally and mentally. When a loved one dies, it's like a piece of your heart was just being ripped or torn out. It's so hard to mend back but you take one step at a time daily until you can come to terms of a deceased loved one being gone. Nobody else in the world can understand the pain that you are going through, it's unexplainable sometimes. You can't even talk about it without breaking down or crying. Sometimes we may even blame ourselves because we did not do all we could for them while they were alive. We may have stopped talking to them because of how they may not have been there for you: just abandoned you while you could have been growing up, gave you up for adoption, abused you physically and sexually, showed favoritism with your brother or sister and not you or introduced you to drugs. You may not have made enough money to help them and that could be eating you up inside; only if you were able to do more instead of less. If you had to help out in the household because you were the oldest, you had to get a job and quit school whereas everyone else got an education because there wasn't enough money in the household to take care of everyone. But at one point in your life you have to come to terms of going forward and letting the past be the past and living for the present and the future and letting the lord direct your steps if you believe and have faith. If you don't believe in the lord, just keeping pressing on or forward; everything heals in time because time is the essence in whatever is bothering you in life. When you think of a deceased loved one, it's hard to think of them gone away for good and never coming back. But as you can remember, mom gave birth to you. There are two things you do in life. That's being born and dying. You can't avoid it. No money in the world can keep you alive when it's your time to go. The first time my great-great-grandmother passed away, I truly missed her. There was no one to call me bad names. Every time I would walk up the sidewalk, she would say here comes that whoa. She would literally embarrass me if I brought my man to meet my family or ask what his name is and call him one of my ex-boyfriend's names on purpose; letting that man know I probably change men like I change my panties or just do not know how to commit to one relationship. It was like I knew what she was going to say to me before she said it. I thought it was just funny. I really miss her. Then my uncle passed away, you know they say death comes in three's. When loved ones die, you do get lonely because part of your family is leaving you and all you have is memories to go on. My uncle was a man full of life: served his country, he loved his children, loved life, worked from sun up until the sun went down, had plenty of children, loved to drink and never been sick a day in his life. Then one day, he was mowing the church grass and had a heart attack and puff he was gone. Then my first cousin passed away. We were close. When you saw him, he always had: a new car every year; not just any car a BMW, Infinity, Mercedes, Lexus and all those top of the line cars; fine designer clothes from head to toe; plenty of women and was married too. The women knew about each other or heard something about one another; even his wife. All of them had kids by him. When he passed away, the wife got to meet his children she never knew he had and his women. It was twisted. He was loved by everyone. The type of cousin you grew up together done everything with as a kid. One you never forget like a piece of your heart cut out. This type of loneliness is like an emptiness torn inside and out. People you are used to being around and seeing every holiday or family reunion is no longer there anymore. You're lonely for their presence; missing that person's physical body around. Then the ultimate death was of my father, who was my dog, best friend and the only one I could count on when I couldn't make it. The one, who would help me financially and always, gave me words of encouragement spiritually. He was gone but that weekend of his death was bizarre. We had a long conversation about his life and mine. He asked me to forgive him of not always being there for me. The choices he made in his life weren't good ones. He wanted me to be happy. That particular day I hugged him and gave him a kiss, not knowing that would be the last time I would see him alive. When they told me he had passed away, I couldn't stand up on my feet. I dropped to the floor with my head in my hands crying loud and louder. My heart felt like it was cut in half. I couldn't believe he was gone. I didn't want to live without my daddy. I felt all alone. I knew I had to do everything on my own now because no one else was going to help me. My mom was living but we weren't close like my dad. She was always jealous of her girls. Always wanting her friends to tell her she was better looking than her daughters. I knew from my end no one else was going to help me but the lord. That's who my dad taught me to rely on if he was not around. But here's the twist that was bizarre. The night before my dad passed away, he came to me. I knew I was asleep. He said, "Wake up little Chaunda." My whole house lit up like a Christmas tree. I had no lights in my living room but it was lit up. He told me he was going away but I had to be there for the family. He would always be with me. Then he turned into a dove and disappeared. It was like I was sleepwalking. I remember getting back into my bed going fast to sleep. But I didn't remember anything until I was told at work that he'd passed away. I thought this was weird. I'm still not over the death of my father but I always visit his gravesite and put fresh flowers there and talk to him giving him an update on me and the rest of the family members. When you lose a loved one, it takes something from you deep inside; causing you to shut others out; causing you to cry from within your soul; causing you to be alone for the rest of your life. As I mentioned over and over, a part of your heart is cut in half because you miss seeing that person alive from day to day. The relationship and closeness you had developed is gone; knowing you have to continue to move on in life without those loved ones. This is my story of a deceased loved one. This is actually the writer's story of a deceased love one; how lonely it has been for me and loneliness creeping inside of me; not having that person around but fond memories left.

SEPARATION

Separation is something that's associated with loneliness. Separation is being apart from your mate, boyfriend, girlfriend or roommate for a period of time. When you are with someone everyday, you get used to that person that you are around on a regular basis. Then for whatever reason, you separate whether due to an argument, drugs, cheating, growing apart from one another, physical abuse, staying out with your friends too long, not helping with paying the bills, nothing in common, or a violent temper. If that person isn't living in the same household as you, you miss that person even though you may not admit it to yourself. Especially if you are used to that person's talks, kisses, lovemaking, arguments, cooking, cleaning, listening to music on the computer or just the way two people kick it together. Now everything you do in your life now is by yourself, alone. Now you eat by yourself, probably talk to yourself, read a book alone, go out clubbing alone, go to the movie alone, go to church by yourself, cook for one person, exercise by yourself, nobody to share the other seat in the car, play Nintendo by yourself and play board games by yourself, think by yourself and phone calls probably limited. Also being separated, leaves you in the house all cooped up by yourself, leaving you feeling lonely and bored to death without the company of a loved one. Missing that person soo soo much that your heart just bleeds inside without the company of a loved one. When you miss a person soo soo much, you spend all your time thinking how to get that person back. Ask yourself if the relationship is salvageable? Can you move on to the next person? Ask yourself if it's your fault. Can I make a change for the better? Will that person come back to me? Will that person stay gone? What about me can I change to make the relationship better? Am I a materialistic person? Is that why I may have lost the one I love? Am I self-centered and selfish? Could that be why we couldn't get alone? Does he/she have the lord in their life? These are some of the questions that come up when two people are separated. When you separated from someone and children are involved, you do need to consider how they may react or feel. The children become lonely and distant without the other mate who is daddy or mommy. Sometimes children may close inside where their communication stops and the children began not to care about anything because their household was a family and now it's not. Sometimes, as individuals, we leave for our own reasons and not think about how this may affect the children that are involved which could leave people going back to each other because of the mode of loneliness creeping up in their child. Once a child is lonely, what do they do? They become distant, not responding to anything you saying, quiet not wanting to study any more or keeping their grades up, interest in anything disappears, keep asking about where mommy or daddy is and blaming you for them leaving. So you end up going back because of the kids but this is okay for their future. Stay until your children can cope. Even if there was problems that existed or you still may leave the mate, girlfriend or boyfriend because the relationship is hopeless which brings about loneliness. When you're at home in that lonely mode sitting in your favorite chair and watching TV, you began to think about that spouse which you separated from; may even think about why you loved that person in the first place; what made that person unique in his/her own way. When you were with your mate, you got to know him/her day by day. It could be that there are some things you don't like about him/her. You start realizing this is not what you want. You began to scrutinize how tidy he/she isn't, his personality whether he/she is nice or mean, the way he/she handles the money or pays the bills, how late he/she stays out and not include you, how he/she really feels about children, whether they want children or not, how he feels about his/her parents are their distance between them or whether or not can he/she keep a job. You realize then that you both had many issues between one another that you never even considered or asked one another about when you were dating until you got married or were living together. But when you separated you realize that you miss that person a lot more than you thought. That's probably why you separated for issues that came up between you two that cause you your loneliness.

Being separated from a person you love can be lonely. The two somehow come together lonely and loneliness. It's hard to get your life back on the right track; without feeling your soul is missing something inside like you bleeding inside without any control; like they say can't stop that feeling. Being separated from someone you love and can't be with that someone will make you cry inside and outside very much emotionally; daily until you try to get over that person. You may even ask yourself what I did to make that person I love leave me. Why we just couldn't get along which caused this empty feeling of loneliness inside of me. Sometimes being separated, just depending on how deep your love is, can cause you to take your own life or attempt to commit suicide or take both of your lives because of being in that lonely state that you feel deep in your soul and mind, that you can't pull it out its just there and won't go away. At that particular time, you don't have any control of what you might do. You may very well snap, that's what loneliness can do to a person being separated from a loved one you desperately miss. What can be a solution when you're separated? Going out and being around people in public places or just start dating someone else can help you get over someone and find something to occupy your mind and time so you won't keep thinking about that person and become scared to date. Just give another person a chance if you do not want to make it with the person you separated from. By all means leave the past in the past and try to move forward not bringing old baggage in a new relationship because it will never work. Because that person treated you bad don't mean the next person will. God could have sent you what you're looking for in a person/mate. Don't forget the support of your family also; such as mom, dad, brother, sister, family, friends or someone close to you. Last but definitely not least is going to the lord in prayer if you are a believer and reading the good book the Bible to help you from a religious standpoint to help you from being lonely and lost in your soul. If you're not religious, just being around people you love and care about can make you feel better inside your heart and soul.

TRIUMPH OF WAR

When you think of war, it's people fighting for their country against one another; what it stands for and its belief. The word war can leave a person disillusioned or lonely for instance. Because you got to go and fight for your country so no other country can come and take over. Then there will not be any more democracy. If you don't, you won't be able to live your life having your freedom. A person can be working; caught up in his career whether it's a doctor, nurse, pharmacist, lawyer, computer technician, farmer, manager, receptionist, administrative assistant, adjuster, secretary, truck driver, stewardess, pilot, cab driver, cashier, bus driver, stock person, mechanic, housewife or etc. You get a letter that Uncle Sam wants you then that person is called in to fight for his/her country, just uprooting their life. Then everything that person just worked for in his/her life has come to a halt. Leaving behind a family such as a wife or husband, girlfriend, boyfriend or lover or common law mate or that person could be leaving his fiancé behind or that person may not be even married for someone to carry on his/her family name. Just the impact of going to war makes you lonely, leaving behind everything that might have meant something to you. When you're dealing with a family saying goodbye, that hurts inside even though you may not show it because you have to be strong and tough. You don't know when you may return telling that girlfriend, boyfriend, husband, wife or whoever meant something special to you goodbye. They're missing you because they're used to seeing you everyday day in and day out and now they don't. This is what loneliness is. Let's break this down. Take for instance, the girlfriend/boyfriend or common law mate you're with two to three years, less or more. Then you're called to go to war or duty. That Uncle Sam wants you. Never being able to marry the person that you fell in love with, you end up leaving that person behind. You think to yourself what a marriage could be like; never getting a chance to experience that in your life; not grabbing that chance; taking advantage of getting married when you were together before you got that letter that Uncle Sam wants you. But you got those fond memories that you have shared while you were together to take with you to war. Now look at a wife/husband for instance, they're married; they're used to being around one another just about everyday of their lives; talking to each other; that person they been with have become in time their best friend/companion. Then they are gone. Then the missing of the other half becomes more prevalent which takes notice in your life which is a form of loneliness. You become lonely for that love person in life. They're no longer around for the time being. They might not make it alive or they could have even survived the outcome of war, which is a blessing. The lord has spared their life. Now life can start again with the other half. If kids are involved, the kids will become lonely also because they will miss seeing their mom or dad off to war; especially talking to them, playing with them, howling or fussing at them when they do wrong or even disciplining them, buying them whatever they want or crave for, just being around them, just having plain fun, reading a children book to them, teaching or helping them with their homework or teaching them to spell their name, watching cartoons or Sesame Street with them or playing basketball, football, baseball, swimming, cooking, sewing or taking them to the ball games—just some of the things that are taken away when mom or dad go to war. With children, they always remember the good things they shared with their parent or parents in their stored memory. Then that military person is off to the triumph of war; going to a strange country not knowing who to trust but only people in your platoon; scared stiff but don't show it or admit it. Now, that military person has to remember the things they were taught to survive in war when they were in training camp; having to lookout for oneself and others while they're in a strange country where people in that country could be their enemy. If that person is at war in the country, that military person will have to use his machine gun, bombs and enough bullets on him/her to keep themselves alive from their enemy and look out for their squad or their group and dodge those bullets, bombs or machine guns that's coming their way; at him/her while one of the military persons is sleeping or fighting for the cause. He/she has to hear gunshots in their sleep. That will wake them up and their survival skills kick in. They maybe fearful to go back to sleep because their lives could be on the line or their partners and others they care about. Every night, he/she will ask themselves if they will make it home alive to see the loved ones they left back home. Lonely thoughts within their hearts and minds of what they left behind and will they ever see them alive again come to mind. When you're lying awake in the jungle or wherever that military person is, you begin to remember, reminisce or wander what it was like to meet their mate for the very first time or their girlfriend/boyfriend or fiancé/fiancée in their minds. If you have no one but mom, dad, grandmother, grandfather, your foster or adoptive parents, you have fond memories that help you to get by. Believe it or not loneliness creeps in when you're away from your homeland. Thank god for memories. A military person is remarkable; one that has to go off and fight for their country leaving behind the ones that means the most to them. But with the courage they have, they do it by keeping prayer foremost in their lives. If they don't have God in their life or if they do not have fond memories to remember, to go on they have their strength and will power they developed within themselves. One thing to always remember, memories, letters and pictures are the key to always having something to focus back on; to keep you going on until you come home. Those that lose your loved ones; it's not the government's fault. They were serving their country; trying to make it safe in our country so we can continue living our everyday normal life. Remember they wanted also a better education and a career. When we are born it's already written in the good book, when we are going to die and how. So whatever you doing, wherever you go and whoever you following you never know when death will come or sneak up on you. Remember no human person has control over death. The triumph of war in fact is a dedication of our troops to keep us free in our country—a country of democracy and equality for all.

RAPE

This is a topic that happens to women, men and children on a daily basis in the United States every second of the hours and minutes of the day. When we think of rape, we think of someone taking someone's body with excessive force and without their permission which is usually true in every circumstance of life. I was lying on the couch and thinking about how a woman is raped and how it would affect her mentally and emotionally. In today's society, this is also happening to boys and men. For example, a woman can be raped if they are at college in a new state: going out with a friend you just may have met at college; both of you go out to a club one night; not knowing one another real good; just want to have some fun; looking good dress from head to toe; had that body working; having the right curves no tummy no fat; just got it together shaped like an hour glass; got that short dress on with your back out and your boobs showing; just attractive; dancing with almost all the men when asked that night; walking around the club over and over; checking the men out; on the dance floor every chance; it's presented to you; having yourself a ball; both you and your friend; then one of you meet a man you want to go home with so your sexual desire can be satisfied; make sure you use an condom while you met this man and left the other person there by oneself. She may not have a way back home. When the club was over, a gentlemen may ask to escort her home or to her car. You accept maybe because you may not have known anyone since you are a stranger in a new state. You could have thought this person was a good person; instead you had to wait for a bus. So he offers to walk with you and wait for the bus to come. He may ask you to walk through an alley so you can get there quicker where it is dark; not thinking you should always walk where there is light. You do it. The man you thought was nice and well dressed in his suit, for asking to walk you to the bus stop, wasn't nice after all. As both of you walk along the alley way, its about three o'clock in the morning and nobody's around. He comes up from behind you and start ripping your clothes off, tearing your stockings, busting your lip, hitting you in your face to get to your insides and start raping you without your permission; no one to call out to save you because it's dark and late. You can't scream because you maybe in shock and stunned by this man's action. The alley way is probably by the club or he could have raped you by a dumpster. Someone may have heard and turned their ears off or just didn't bother to do anything to help you. After he finished what he wanted, he leaves you there with nothing on you. Being in shock, you probably stayed where you were for hours until you had the strength to get up and piece your clothes together and catch the bus. You got on the bus; people looking at you strange. You feel eyes roving about all on you. But you're not in your right stable mind. You arrive back at college in your dormitory. You wash and clean yourself up, not even calling your parents or calling the police or filing charges. When you saw your friend, you didn't even tell her; going through your everyday routine putting what happened to you in the back of your mind; not facing it like it never even happened to you; thinking that you can cope with rape yourself, alone; withdrawing yourself from everyone around you; drawing up or climbing up inside of yourself; being scared of men but not facing what happened to you. Not only that, you become lonely in your life you let loneliness creep up inside your soul deep down; not aware of it. See, when you are raped there's fear that sets in you. You won't tell someone thinking you can handle it own your own. No one can handle rape on their own. When it happens to you whether you are a female or male, then there are questions you may ask yourself in your mind. What did I do to deserve this to happen to me? Why or why me? Why did he pick me out of the rest? Were my clothes too provocative or see though? Did he think I was easy? Did he notice I was by myself? Did he have too much to drink and was not aware of what he was doing to me? Was I tipsy? Should I have stayed home until I really knew somebody or made friends at my school before I went out to a club? Was this just my fault? Why didn't I walk where there was light? Was I just at the wrong place at the wrong time? Why couldn't I scream for help? Why didn't I have some type of spray or something to protect myself? Why couldn't I just tell somebody? You think to yourself, I just only wanted to have some fun. I didn't want to stay on campus by myself. I was just trying to make some friends since I'm in a strange state I thought. I didn't want to sit at home alone feeling lonely inside. By not coping with rape, you may tend to eat your problems away gaining hundreds of pounds, being scared of men, not wanting to go outside or anywhere that you can enjoy yourself thinking it can happen again. Sometimes you may need to talk to a psychiatrist to deal with rape or your ordeal because nine out of ten; if it happens once, it can happen again. If you're close to your mom, talk to her about the rape, how deeply it scared you, how you can cope and move on with your life. Just report this to the police if you can remember what he looks like so he can pay the price for raping you so it won't happen to someone else. When you get the needed help, you can cope with what happened to you; you can become you again, having no fear of anything. You see, rape can cause you to withdraw yourself from others, being at a distance causes you to trap yourself in a shell that only you can come out of. This is a part of loneliness. Sometimes no one can help you but you. I just wanted to say to the person that's raping someone when you get to a point in life that you have to rape someone get a grip on yourself, pray and ask God to take this away from you right then. Remove it from your heart and mind. It can be done. All you need is self-control; instead of committing a crime and going to jail where someone is going to rape you for doing it to someone else. Before you get to prison, they already know the crime you committed. They will take revenge for that person you raped. Even if you don't believe in God, pray anyway not to hurt someone and go the opposite way from that person you want to rape. Recognize your problem; staying in awareness or control of yourself. Don't let loneliness draw you into a web of ugliness. I hate to say this but if you need to rape someone in fear of being lonely, you need sex or some company go pickup a prostitute on the street instead of hurting someone so innocent and pure. Ask yourself, what if this was my daughter or son being raped by someone how would I feel if this happened to them? How would my wife, daughter or son feel if they knew I was a rapist?

HOLIDAY SEASON

It's that time of the year again when October gets here then Thanksgiving and Christmas. That's the time you become zealous and joyous, looking forward to the holidays. This is the time you get to see everybody you haven't seen during the year or years. For Thanksgiving, you get a chance to see all your uncles, aunts, cousins and close friends whom you haven't seen all year. You meet at somebody's house to give thanks and praise for what God has blessed you with during the prosperous year. But for some, they have nobody to share, gather with or mingle with during Thanksgiving holiday. Sometimes they care not to be. They may be at home all alone, no good food to eat, laughs or talks with family and friends. Yet they may end up crying because they're eating all alone and feeling empty inside and sad. People move from other states due to a job transfer. They may never return to where they used to live or where their family live causing them to be lonely around the holidays. They may not have enough money to go back home or no transportation to get there or they just do not care to go back to where they grew up. Sometimes there are no fond memories to remember. They spend the holidays alone and lonely where loneliness creeps in, of course. Then there are some who live in the same city or state with their family but are distant from them, having no contact with any of their family members for various reasons causing them to be alone again on the holidays. Even if you ask people around you or in your neighborhood each person would have a story to tell why they're distant or don't visit their family for the holidays. Being lonely around the holidays isn't good for any person's sake. In your mind you think it's okay but actually it is not. Whatever reason you have cannot be so bad you can't pick up the phone and just say happy Thanksgiving or merry Christmas or send a postcard or Christmas card. Had you thought about what if that person passed away? You never took the time to mend fences or wish that person a happy holiday season every year or just to say hello or please forgive me or I apologize for whatever happened between us and move on. It just takes seconds to do, it doesn't hurt. We really need to be around people and say hello which will keeps us out of that loneliness mode. Remember loneliness is something that creeps deep inside your soul and you don't know how to get rid of that feeling. Loneliness may make you think crazy and do things you have no control of; at that time depends on your state of mind. Around the holiday season, a lot of people become distant; not sociable be in their own world leaving them feeling sorry for themselves and wanting to commit suicide, cut themselves up with a knife/razor blade like punishing themselves because they're not around anyone. Being at home by themselves, they ask why I have no one to share the holiday season with. When you're by yourself you usually go into deep thought; thinking about everything you have gone through in life; thinking about the good times and the bad times; thinking about the things that make one cry or want to take their own life whether by taking pills, shooting yourself in the head with a gun, cutting your wrist until you bleed to death. All this is part of loneliness because sometimes when loneliness creeps in you act out. Everybody loves the holiday season. Sometimes holiday season may not love us. For Christmas, this is the time of the season for giving and being joyous. Some people feel that if they can't give a gift or money around the holiday especially Christmas which is the gift giving time, they'd rather be at home by themselves feeling empty, lonely and blue inside. When people don't have the money to buy gifts to give to their friends and family, they may charge them on their credit cards to the max or write hot checks to pay for the gifts; money they don't even have. All of the above is sometimes done out of impulse because you're in the Christmas spirit. This right here can put pressure on you to buy, buy and buy when it's around Christmas time. If you don't have any money to buy gifts, you can withdraw yourself from others around the Christmas holidays not wanting to come around because you don't have a gift to give. But always remember Christmas is the time to be thankful that Jesus was born. He gave his life so we can have eternal life free from sin. Gifts or money can't buy you eternal life, only Christ Jesus can give you this. That's what Christmas is all about. Jesus definitely is the reason for the season; not gift buying or gift giving. None of those gifts is going to give you eternal life. When Christmas time is here, we'll always be thinking wrong in our little heads. What did somebody get me for Christmas? Who gave what? Who was together or not? Who looked like a hot mess? Who looked like they were drunk or on crack? Who all came? What were they wearing? What dish did they bring? When you feel like this, you should automatically just go visit to get the scoop for yourself. Ask yourself what it will hurt. Nothing? You should just ignore that person who may have talked about you because each individual is accountable to the lord for their own salvation. If a person talks about you and says things that are not true about you, we all have haters in the family. During the holidays some family members let you know how they really feel about you; not taking your feelings into consideration. Love them in your heart even if they don't love you. Some may try every year to get a gift or buy a gift. Their plan may fail not due to their fault just due to some unforeseen circumstances that happen all of a sudden. We must remember whatever we do for someone whether it's buying a gift or exchanging a gift we should do everything in love; not expecting anything in return. That person is already feeling bad because they could not buy that person anything. Once that person leaves your house not being able to buy a gift for anyone, that person could very well drive their car off the road, take their own life, set their own house on fire, jump into a swimming pool and try to drown themselves. Christmas or any holiday can have you sad sometimes feeling empty inside bringing about loneliness leaving you all alone deep in your soul. My uncle used to drink his holiday away until Christmas was over because it was a sad time of the year for him. All his loved ones were deceased. This doesn't solve anything, the issue is still there. So whatever comes in your life, you must try to deal with it right then or head on. You're stronger than you give yourself credit for. You just don't know it but you are. Christmas should be a time when everyone is happy but it's not always. It's the lonely time of the season. You know what, I feel could help a person during any holiday season, keeping Christ's first in your life in everything you say and do and read the Bible. If you don't feel you have time to read, just get the bible on DVD. Please remember whatever gift you give should come from your heart; not expecting anything in return. That's all any one person can do. Always remember what's the reason for the season in Christmas christ was born, christ died for our sins so we can have eternal life that's reality; not gift giving that comes once a year. Christ comes everyday and all day long. What a glorious precious gift God gave us.

FINANCIAL DIFFICULTY

This type of topic affects just about almost everyone sometime or another in life. Having money problems, it's nothing like being depressed when you don't have enough money to pay your bills. You know, bill collectors constantly harassing you by phone calling you for past due amounts because bills have not been paid on time or not at all. Financial difficulty is like swimming without a paddle because you don't know where you're going to come up with all this money and where you going to get it from. You might have to file bankruptcy; paying your bills through a caseworker that's assigned to you by the judge. You might have to result to penny-pinching your bills, such as paying a little portion of your bills until next month or just enough to get by so nothing won't get cut off. Then just sometimes you might have to get a payday loan or a loan to pay all your bills for the month. You don't have all the money to pay your bills, resulting in a financial difficulty. Don't think you're the only one that has done this, you are not alone. They just don't let you know. There are a lot of us doing this on a regular basis. They may not talk about it to you but they have done it. Trying to pay bills or make ends meet sometimes can become so very tedious. It's a routine, every week, every other week or once a month. A must situation, if not you will be homeless with no place to live. When there appears to be a problem handling money, you can seem to fall off the face of the earth because you began to withdraw yourself from everybody. You can't keep up financially; paying your bills because money becomes tight causing you to put yourself on a budget. When you don't have enough money, you got to sit back and think, maybe even scrutinizing where you went wrong in your spending habits. Ask yourself, what do I need to stop doing just until I get caught up and getting it under control? Meaning maybe I need to give up going out to dinner, clubs, parties, social events, concerts, plays, museums, zoo, mall, lunch with co-workers, can't buy videos or music, no more subscription for the weekly paper or magazines, no more buying new furniture or big screen TV's, stereo system, DVD's, beer, alcohol, buying make up to make up your face, becoming limited because your pocketbook has become small, got to get real, no getting a refill on your nails or pedicure for your toes or just a plain manicure, filling your gas tank up with only five or ten dollars here and there to make it during the week, your tithes for the church may change where you were giving one percent of your salary now you can only give fifty, twenty dollars maybe one dollar that's all you have until you can get back on your feet. This is what happens to a person when money problems come into play. You got to budget budget budget (bbb). When this happens to you, it draws you in a shell of your own into seclusion deep in your soul withdrawing from everyone; not socializing like you use to do; causing you to stay home and not answering the phone. Someone knocks at your door, you won't answer the door. What is this? Loneliness! Because you got bills, bills, and more bills. A connection hun. Sometimes when you have money problems you lose all your friends. Your friends no longer treat you like they used to, leaving you hurt. To their despair, your friends might want to call you but in the back of their minds you do not have any money so they call another friend that can financially go; drawing you to become lonely within. Having no friends around sometimes can draw you into a pity party, feeling sorry for yourself because when you have financial difficulties you have all the financial woes and headaches that comes with being broke. When we have financial difficulties, it does bring about stress in our lives which can bring on health issues such as ulcers, heart attacks, irregular heartbeats, headaches and could even bring about cancer or maybe if you have cancer, it could spread quickly because you're worried about getting those bills paid. Financial difficulties can bring about divorce or separation with your spouse, woman friend or man friend because maybe your spouse can't provide you with the things you're used to having or he/she can't pay the bills or buy your wants which can be described as money, clothes, jewelry, trips, movies, eating at the finest restaurant, a new car, getting your hair done and concerts. Financial difficulties can bring about unhappiness in your life because everything may not go right with you. You have one money problem after another. Bills, bills, bills causing you to be sad stuck up in the house all the time; don't want to go anywhere; too broke to do anything. Sometimes most people can't handle not having any money. Some people often take their own lives or just become homeless because of the everyday struggle and pressure that comes with living on a daily basis; getting up every morning, going to work for forty hours a week, paying those bills again, foremost going to church to keep your sanity but this is life sometimes you have to deal with the good and bad that come with financial difficulties. Let's keep it real, maybe it's a test to bring you back to the lord or to get closer with the lord. When you have money problems, everything goes wrong or end up happening all at one time causing you not to think straight. Oftentimes, you end up making good decisions or bad choices when it comes down to paying your bills. When money problems occur one after another: here comes car problems, go to work one day then find out you're being laid off causing you to get evicted from your place of residence and your vehicle getting repossessed. Once this happens, keep the faith, don't go into that shell or cry all day long. Just remember second Corinthians 12:13, don't let your bills become a burden to you. Remember one thing, what mom and dad have always told you growing up, to save for a rainy day open up a savings at a credit union. When you get paid each pay period, put some money in like fifteen dollars every time you get paid cause this add up and every little bit helps. When you do this, don't withdraw any money out. Just treat the account like it was not there or existing at all. Just keep putting money in and watch it grow. This might help you try it because it just could help. Then one more thing, write all your bills down in a tablet that's due that month. Once you get paid, if it's once a month or every two weeks, make sure the bills you wrote down is what you pay when you get paid. If you can't pay them all, just pay what you can and get an extension on the rest of the bills if you can. When buying anything, ask yourself do I need this or is this just a want that I have? If it's a want you can leave that where it is. Buying your wants sometime is what leads you into a financial difficulty. What you see you want is not always what you can afford. Just focus on your needs and not your wants. This will help you stay on that straight road path to be bill free. In other words, you only have necessity bills which are light bill, house payment or rent, telephone, car note, car insurance and cable. When you get here, you are out of your financial difficulty.

AGING

When we, as individuals, reach a certain age in our life, like coming age of thirty or forty, we feel our life is over and we want to be young again. We go buy all this type of cream for our face to enhance our inner beauty and hide the wrinkles. We also exercise everyday; trying to tone the fat so we won't have rolls of fat in our tummy that other people can see. Then we get us some new bodies, surgery to flatten our tummy or surgery to take the fat off all the areas in our body. We want people to tell us how young we look but we know we are getting older. We want to dress like we were in our twenties; such as wearing mini skirts, jerri curls, tight clothes, different hats, going clubbing where we shake our booty; thinking we can party until one o'clock or two o'clock in the morning. But our bodies have changed. We need to recognize this; that each age we mature too we want to become that person which we are in that age range such as dressing our age, loving ourselves, being what you are and happy. This is also type of loneliness of hiding behind a mirror or hiding within your inner self not accepting who you are and where you are in your life. Loneliness is longing to be a certain way inside or outside not feeling or being comfortable with yourself. When we age, we are no longer looked at the same; like being trapped within your body and no way out. A sense of loneliness because the game out in the world has changed. The men don't look at you the same. We look old to them, less sex appealing. Our clothes don't fit right, they're too tight. We gain weight and spread in your hips. Our faces have dark spots under them. Our wrinkles are more noticeable. We're not a size seven or ten anymore. We may become a fourteen through twenty-two plus sizes. If we wear something tight, it doesn't look cute on us because the clothing doesn't go with our age. Accepting how our body is changing becomes weird. We can't keep our mate because if we are married the spouse may look elsewhere for that vibrant feeling they used to get or the thin woman they used to have around. Loneliness creeps in because we just don't feel right within us something missing we just don't know how to describe it. When we begin to age in our course of life we stop partying in those dance clubs. We begin to play golf, tennis, bike riding, going to movies, getting closer to God, going to church more often than we did before, Bible study or being more active doing more roles, taking up more duties or responsibilities in the church house. We develop more patience with ourselves, go out to eat more even if it's by yourself. Our bodies don't crave for sex all the time like when we were younger where we craved for sex all the time. Nowadays, if we sleep with someone we are engaging in protected sex not unprotected sex. We learn to deal with getting to know ourselves; not jumping into relationships right after one breaks up, like jumping into the skillet into the frying pan. We tend to read more books, take our lives more seriously going after our credentials, that degree we always wanted but never had the time to get, getting our certification, going back to school to take a trade or seeking another profession. Positive note, as we age life makes more sense than it ever did before. But as we age we become less likely to take risks in our lives; just settling for whatever. When you age your mate doesn't see you the way you used to be; like a size four, six, eight or ten or beautiful. But time has brought about a change. You've spread out, wrinkles develop and gray hair has appeared and fat stays on your body; something that you have to get used to and let age grow on you. Like who you are because if you don't you could go into a dark secretive web of loneliness not accepting what you become in time and caught up in a world of which you're not anymore. I'm talking about the men too. Men feel the same way like women. Aging is a wonderful thing, you can look back at the day when you were younger and compare how you do things now. For the most part, people in general whether stay as they are now because their views and perspective are different than when they were younger. You can see the failure and hardships that you did in your past because you were young. As you age, you try not to make those mistakes you once did. You may want to ask yourself is there life after thirty or forty? Yes, there surely is. That doesn't mean you rush off to get married because you don't want to become an old maid. You should be patient because no matter what age you are, love will always find you. Where loneliness exists, it doesn't have to creep in and draw you into a shelter excluding yourself from anybody because of your age. There are a lot of places to see and lot of things to do that's every bit of wholesome for you or your spouse or friend. Always be happy with yourself and be confident in you because no one else can do this for you. As you age your body changes, accept it. Age gracefully and with dignity because age brings about wisdom which can help others from your own life experiences and always be able to give words of encouragement to steer others in the right path. This will help you to deal with you aging; knowing someone else may need you and you can advise or inspire others leaving loneliness no way to creep inside of you.

CONCLUSION

Being alone sometimes is not always associated with loneliness if you are content with yourself. Loneliness means you missing someone, you're not whole or complete yet. There's something lacking within you deep inside your soul. You can't figure it out. Say what? Loneliness is not designed to help everyone who read this book. Some might say loneliness is not present but if loneliness is present in you some kind of way and how it comes into your mind with a question mark. Then you fit into this category. Sometimes loneliness can cause you to make decisions, choices that affect the whole outcome in life. You don't know why you do the things you do and make those crazy decisions in your life. When loneliness comes into play, you do some crazy stuff or foolish things in your life; never thinking about what you doing or scrutinizing what you doing, just doing it. We really need to get back to thinking, using that brain of ours, bringing us up against that thought process: meaning, scrutinizing that decision or that choice that we decided on that may affect the whole outcome in life because we can't go back and correct that bad choice or decision we made but move forward and try to do better. I hope this book is a wake up call to you yourself. Recognizing the signs, state of mind you in when loneliness sweeps you up can often becomes a behavior pattern. Stop look and pay attention to yourself. Then this book might be designed to help you. I, the writer, tried to touch such topics that loneliness is associated with in your life. I may not have touched a lot of other areas that loneliness comes into play but I hope I was thorough in writing some topics that you thought about in your gut but didn't know how to express yourself to anyone not even your psychiatrist. The reason for writing this book is to help someone to recognize if they have this type of issue in their life; how they can help themselves become a better person rather than act out. When you think about loneliness, you can become trapped in a spider web trying to find your way out so you can become a better you by improving areas in your life that needs attention. My late father, the Reverend Michael Pradia, always tried to help everyone he came in contact with even if that meant giving others the clothes off his back, making sure children in need had their shots, school supplies, food or a place to stay. He was an awesome Methodist minister; always caring and showing love to everyone he came into contact with. I was just happy to be his daughter. He always tried to help people in general. I thought maybe I'd write this book to help someone that may feel trapped by loneliness and may not know how to recognize the signs or related symptoms. My book is dedicated to my daddy, the late Reverend Michael Pradia in Houston, Texas. May he rest in peace, love from his darling daughter. I hope I'm able to help someone, I know I can't help everybody but reading this book may touch somebody life and just maybe they will change some kind of way. I feel this book is an inspirational self help book. Life is always a journey. We may not know it but it is. Once we've gone through our journey in life then our life becomes clear and more on a routine basis. We have to make the most of loneliness in our lives. Sometimes if you're in this situation, always have joy in your life, be happy inside of you even if loneliness is present. Find happiness in things you do for you. Elevate your mind, heart and soul to do and think good. Don't make hasty decisions in your life because no one is around to love or to share your love with or be in love or get in love with. Love is a wonderful combination. You only live once, remember you hold the key to turn everything around in your life to positive instead of negative. I want to thank my mom who always said this book was just a pipe dream of mine and I was living in a dream world. Don't let anyone stop you from dreaming and trying to make your dream come true. Every one of us has a gift that nobody else has but you. My mom also would tell me throughout my life god bless a child that got its own. This just made me strive extra harder to make my dreams come true with the help of the good lord above. I want to thank my precious two daughters for their loving support and encouraging words to me. I want to thank my longtime boo Sheila for always being there for me no matter what when nobody else was. Thanks Sheila for always having my back in my life. I want to thank Lisa for her TV stand to sit my typewriter on to type. I really was down on my luck. I want to thank A D for buying my typewriter to type my book. I want to thank Debra for feeding me, she always had insight if I was hungry or not. I want to thank Macy's in WillowBrook for hiring me part-time so that I could update my wardrobe and learn about fashion. I want to thank Karen for always saying "drive your bus girl". I want to thank my pastor, Reverend Samuel Ammons in Houston, Texas for helping me to learn more about God's word and developing a personal and deep relationship with god and keeping Christ first in my life. I want to thank my financial backer who the lord brought into my life to put me back on my feet. What an awesome individual. I want to thank the good lord above because of him this book is possible. Thanks be to the lord for carrying me through all the storms, test and trials in my life safely and never leaving me but always right on time in working every situation out when I least expected it throughout my entire life. I hope all my new found readers and fans enjoy this book "Say What? Loneliness".

POEM FOR YOUR THOUGHTS

Loneliness can open the door and close the door in your life today.

Loneliness can make you feel depress and low.

Loneliness can take you on a journey you never knew. High lows and low highs.

Loneliness can make you do things you thought you would never do. Stay focused and true to you.

If you make a mistake along the way count your blessing and let god show you the way.

Evil thoughts and evildoers can be overcome if you let god show you the just way.

Loneliness can be cold as the morning dew. Always feel your heart with joy and laughter.

Loneliness so sad so gleam so blue. Keep happy those days can be few. Let god take control of those fears that's haunting you.

Let sunshine in and loneliness can poff like it was never known.

A TRIBUTE TO THE LATE REVEREND MICHAEL PRADIA

Cloud in the sky

When you look up to the cloud
In the sky
You feel peace, serenity, surrounds our called ones.
Our loved one was here
In front of us, with us, behind us on the left on the right
Now they're gone look up to the cloud in the sky
Cloud is invisible
You can look right through it there's where the lord has called them to be.
They didn't catch a bus, nor drove a car, nor rode a train
God came, flew them away in that invisible white cloud in the sky
When our love one is gone god will give you the strength and comfort
To move on
Just look up to the cloud in the sky

www.ingramcontent.com/pod-product-compliance
Lightning Source LLC
LaVergne TN
LVHW041540060526
838200LV00037B/1068